POD for Profit
More on the NEW Business of Self Publishing

— Aaron Shepard —

CreateSpace uses it. Lulu.com uses it. So do AuthorHouse, iUniverse, Xlibris, and almost every other self publishing company in the U.S., Canada, and the U.K.

What is it? Lightning Source, the printer and distributor at the heart of the "print on demand" industry. For the work those companies can't handle themselves, it's Lightning they most often depend on.

So, why pay a middleman? In this follow-up to his groundbreaking book *Aiming at Amazon,* Aaron Shepard explores how to double your profit by working directly with Lightning. If you're serious about making money with POD publishing, this book can show you the way.

> "Aaron Shepard is the undisputed expert at earning profit from POD. Here are the step-by-step instructions for setting up your own publishing operation and optimizing the financial benefits. Following Aaron's steps, you will earn two or three times as much per book."
>
> **Bruce Batchelor, author, *Book Marketing DeMystified,* and founder and former CEO, Trafford Publishing**

> "A graduate course and definitive guide for advanced POD publishing."
>
> **Morris Rosenthal, author, *Print-on-Demand Book Publishing***

"Aaron Shepard is exceptional in his ability to keep up with the ever-changing minutiae of the world of self publishing via POD. I wouldn't want to publish without this book within reach."

John Culleton, Wexford Press

"Remarkably thorough and readable."

Jonathan LeBlanc Roberts, Breton Bay Publishing

"Invaluable advice for any small press or independent publishing firm."

Max Scratchmann, Poison Pixie Publishing

"Could not be more timely or helpful. What a wealth of information . . . and not just what to do, but HOW."

Malcolm Dell, Elbow Grease Publishing

"A tremendous amount of information that will benefit an author who self publishes not only through Lightning Source but by any other method."

Kevin Sivils, author, *Self-Publishing with Amazon's CreateSpace*

"I wish I had read a book like this before I started publishing."

Brandon Simpson, Small Town Press

"Lots of valuable, easy-to-understand information. I will recommend this highly to my self-publishing clients as a reference for their many questions. Even after more than a decade in the business, I learned a few things from this book."

Jamie Saloff, Saloff Enterprises

"Another gold mine of information from Aaron Shepard. Absolutely required reading for any self publisher."

Christy Pinheiro, author, *The Step-By-Step Guide to Self-Publishing for Profit!*

"Indispensable if you are considering printing your book POD. Covers every aspect of the process in depth."

Norma Lehmeier Hartie, Lingham Press

"Following Aaron's *Aiming at Amazon* and *Perfect Pages,* his new book completes the tool belt allowing small press entrepreneurs to succeed. Learn the elements essential to flourishing as a publisher—and not just any kind—a profitable one!"

Thomas Hollowell, Undiscovered Press

"Don't go into publishing without it."

Grace Bridges, Splashdown Books

Also by Aaron Shepard

Aiming at Amazon
The NEW Business of Self Publishing

Perfect Pages
Self Publishing with Microsoft Word

The Business of Writing for Children
An Award-Winning Author's Tips on
Writing Children's Books and Publishing Them

POD for Profit

More on the
NEW Business of Self Publishing

OR

How to Publish Your Books
With Online Book Marketing and
Print on Demand by Lightning Source

Aaron Shepard

Shepard Publications
Friday Harbor, Washington

Author portrait by Wendy Edelson, www.wendyedelson.com

ISBN 978-0-938497-46-2

Library of Congress Control Number: 2009911873
Library of Congress subject headings:
Self-publishing
On-demand printing
Lightning Source (Firm)
Books—Marketing

Note: Aaron regrets he cannot provide private guidance in self
publishing. For additional resources, please see "Where to Get
Help" in the appendix.

Version 1.0

Contents

About This Book

This book is both new and not new. It grew out of my earlier book, *Aiming at Amazon,* and some of the material you'll read here was once part of that other book.

Aiming at Amazon outlined the *new* business of self publishing, based on producing and distributing books through print on demand and marketing those books through online booksellers, especially Amazon.com. When the book first came out, there was only one way for a self publisher to profitably approach Amazon—through the POD provider called Lightning Source. So, I treated the two as inseparable elements of my model.

Less than two years later, when the book came up for revision, things had changed. Amazon's own POD offerings had evolved, and its CreateSpace had become a viable alternative for self publishers. Lightning was still the more profitable choice, but CreateSpace, with its greater ease and convenience, was better suited to many beginners. At the same time, I had about three times as much to say about Amazon marketing.

So, the second version of *Aiming at Amazon* focused more on Amazon itself, and I saved most of my remaining content for a second volume to be focused on Lightning Source.

This is that second volume. And like my writing on Amazon marketing, this material too has about tripled in bulk. I've gone into much greater detail about how Lightning works and how to work with it, as well as about other services important to Lightning publishers.

I believe I've been fair and balanced in my discussion of Lightning, but there's no question you'll find praise and admiration for it in these pages. So, let me make clear that I have no official connection to Lightning except as a publisher client. This book is not sponsored by Lightning, and I have neither sought nor received its endorsement.*

Instead, it is based on my own experience with Lightning, which goes back to 1998—only about a year after the company's founding, when it was still called Lightning *Print*. I was among the first self publishers to work with the company, or even to know about it. Since then, I've published almost two dozen books through Lightning. And though I've worked also with BookSurge, CreateSpace, and Replica Books (now TextStream), sales through Lightning provide the bulk of my income today.

Despite growing competition, daunting requirements, and burdensome procedures, Lightning Source remains the prime choice for most modern self publishers determined to maximize profit. If you wish to make a living or earn significant income from your publishing, and if you're capable of clearing the hurdles, then Lightning is your best bet for reaching your goals.

Of course, not all Lightning publishers make money, but many do, and our ranks are growing. For a very rough idea of what's possible, here are the results of a 2008 poll of Yahoo's pod_publishers group—a gathering point for Lightning publishers worldwide—with 28 members responding. Dollar amounts are average monthly *profit* from POD sales, given in U.S. dollars.

---

* I'm grateful, though, for the comments of Lisa Horak, Lightning's Marketing Manager, on a draft of this book, as well as for its review by an unnamed member of the "Ops team."

29%	$0–$100
29%	$100–$1,000
25%	$1,000–$5,000
11%	$5,000–$10,000
4%	$10,000–$50,000
4%	$50,000–$100,000
0%	Over $100,000

The respondents most successful with Lightning would have published multiple titles in nonfiction—reflecting a truth about self publishing in general. Fiction by an unknown author is almost always a harder sell.

By the way, do join our group. You can sign up at

groups.yahoo.com/group/pod_publishers

It's a great place to get ongoing help. (If you're asking about a problem with a particular published book, be sure to identify it to help in troubleshooting.)

Though I can't offer private consulting on publishing, I welcome your feedback, which may help me improve future versions of this book. Please bring your comments and suggestions to my Publishing Page at

www.newselfpublishing.com

Visit that site also for updates to this book, especially in my Publishing Blog. And while you're there, be sure to sign up for my email bulletin to receive notice of important changes and additions.

Though this book is about publishing for profit, I do not consider profit a sufficient reason to publish a book. For me, publishing is a personal process, almost a sacred one— the sharing of worthwhile ideas, helpful information, useful techniques, resources for understanding, and hopefully at times a touch of delight—all from mind to mind, for the betterment of both reader and writer. Yes, profit is important to me, but mainly as a way to enable this process—it allows me to keep publishing.

There are many motives for publishing, and I know this book will be used in support of them all. But if, like me, you see publishing not only as a source of personal enrichment but also as a form of service, then this book has been written for you.

Review the Rules

The *new* business of self publishing is based on a number of principles laid out in my earlier book, *Aiming at Amazon*. For details on most of them, I refer you to that book—but here's a brief recap.

• **Forget bookstores.** This was and is the first principle of this publishing system. As much as we may love bookstores, they are generally not a friendly environment for self publishers, and for very good reasons. Even if you can convince some bookstores to carry your books, you're not likely to sell many copies there. On the other hand, the rise of online booksellers, and particularly Amazon, affords wonderful and unique opportunities that can greatly improve your chances of success.

• **Print on demand.** The new technology of print on demand—POD for short—makes it possible to print and bind books in numbers as low as a single copy. So, self publishing no longer requires buying a garage-full of books, or in fact any books at all, and a title can be published for a much lower initial outlay than ever before possible. At the same time, most companies offering access to this technology also offer distribution well beyond the hopes of most earlier self publishers.

• **Optimize for Amazon.** Self publishers do best when they tailor their books to the opportunities available. With POD books sold online, that means designing elements like titles and book covers specially for online sales. It also generally means publishing nonfiction on topics that book buyers are likely to search for. (If you're publishing fiction, POD might still be part of a larger strategy, but I recommend focusing on ebooks, which allow much more attractive pricing.)

• **Channel your sales.** Though you want your book to be available in as many places as possible, you want as many buyers as possible to get it from Amazon. That's because Amazon rewards a book's popularity with ever-increasing promotion. Start the ball rolling, and Amazon will happily take over from you.

• **Go global.** With POD and online bookselling, your books will be available around the world. Given that advantage, a little special attention to your content and your marketing can bring significant sales in a number of countries.

Now let's take a close look at how Lightning Source fits into the picture.

1
Learning About Lightning

Get the Facts

When self publishers first hear about Lightning Source Inc., they tend to think it's just one more provider of POD author services—or "self publishing company," as these businesses are commonly called—like Lulu.com, AuthorHouse, iUniverse, or Xlibris.

But Lightning is not a "self publishing company" at all, and its services are not aimed at authors. Instead, it aims to serve publishers, and in that role, it has become the very heart of the POD industry. Founded in 1997, Lightning is the company that self publishing companies turn to for much of their book printing and distribution. Even Amazon's CreateSpace offers "expanded distribution" through Lightning as a way to reach other booksellers.

Lightning's print operations are truly massive, and expanding rapidly. By early 2010, Lightning's U.S. and U.K. branches were printing 1.5 million books a month, in print runs averaging 1.8 copies per title. Its complete catalog totaled 1.6 million titles from over 11,000 publishing clients—many of them self publishing companies but most of them individual publishers, from Shepard Publications to Simon & Schuster.

As a distributor, Lightning's importance and effectiveness in the U.S. are largely due to a unique advantage: It's part of the same company that houses Ingram Book Company, the biggest U.S. book wholesaler. Almost all bookstores in the country, as well as many libraries and schools, order books from Ingram.*

---

* In this book, I'll use "Ingram" to refer to Ingram Book Company rather than to either of the Ingram-branded entities encompassing both the wholesaler and Lightning Source. For a family tree, see the special section "The Ingram Companies" later in this book.

As you might expect, Lightning and Ingram work together closely. In fact, Ingram "carries" every title printed by Lightning—even if Ingram doesn't really keep the title in stock. Actually, it may stock some popular Lightning titles, but any others can be printed by Lightning within four hours and delivered to Ingram the next morning, ready for shipping. So, if a bookstore inquires, Ingram reports any Lightning title as immediately available. Any book handled by Lightning, then, can be obtained easily and quickly by booksellers throughout the U.S.

Foremost among U.S. booksellers that can get your book from Ingram is Amazon.com. And because Amazon feeds directly on data sent electronically by both Lightning and Ingram, you are nearly guaranteed that Amazon will list your book. What's more, because Amazon regularly uses Ingram to "drop ship" books direct to customers, Lightning books are normally listed on Amazon as in stock and available with one-day shipping, even if Amazon doesn't have its own copies at the time.*

The connection between Lightning and the rest of the U.S. book trade is even stronger than that. A few huge booksellers have the resources to tap into Lightning's electronic systems and order directly instead of going through Ingram. Here are some of them. (For more, see "Lightning Source Partners" following this section.)

• Baker & Taylor, the second largest U.S. book wholesaler and the largest supplier to U.S. schools and libraries. It is also the primary wholesale supplier to Borders and Borders.com.

---

* Amazon announced in 2008 it would stop selling POD books not produced through its own services but officially backed off from this in November 2009. In any case, this policy was aimed at self publishing companies and publishers of substantial size and never in any way affected independent self publishers working directly with Lightning Source.

• NACSCORP, another major wholesaler, as a service of the National Association of College Stores.

• Barnes & Noble, including BN.com.

• And of course, Amazon.com. Though Amazon normally orders from Ingram to fill immediate customer demand, it often orders direct from Lightning to stock a book in its own warehouses.

Meanwhile, Lightning's overseas branch, Lightning Source UK, is similarly well connected. Among the companies it supplies are Gardners Books and Bertrams|THE—the two biggest U.K. book wholesalers—plus Amazon.co.uk. (Again, for more, see "Lightning Partners" following this section.) Books handled by Lightning in the U.S. can easily be earmarked for printing and distribution by Lightning UK as well—and vice versa.

As Lightning's U.S. and U.K. operations continue to grow, so does its international reach in general. Books printed in those two countries are already available from online booksellers around the world—both in countries that speak English and in countries that don't—including Amazon sites in Canada, France, Germany, and Japan.* Some books are exported by wholesalers or retailers that order direct from Lightning—such as Amazon.com and Ingram's export arm, Ingram International—and others by Lightning itself.

Lightning is also looking to expand the number of countries in which it is based. Australia and Southeast Asia have been considered for new branches. A new center in France, operated in conjunction with the French publisher Hachette Livre, is due to open in 2010.

---

* In late 2009, Brian Dana Akers of YogaVidya.com identified 94 online booksellers worldwide carrying Lightning Source books and guessed there might be two or three dozen more.

In yet another area of expansion, Lightning has become part of an entirely different distribution channel. Through an agreement with On Demand Books, Lightning is among the companies supplying files for printing on the Espresso Book Machine, a small-scale POD press aimed at use by individual bookstores, libraries, and other local businesses and services. (For more on the Espresso, see the special section "The Espresso Book Machine" at the end of this chapter.)

Lightning Source Partners

Here is Lightning's list of wholesalers and retailers that have accounts for direct ordering as of November 2009, with later additions of my own. For the currently posted list plus links to Web sites, visit Lightning Source and click on "Read more" under "Global Distribution Channels," or go direct to

**www.lightningsource.com/
globalDistChannels.aspx**

For Lightning US:
Ingram Book Company
Amazon.com
Baker & Taylor
Barnes & Noble
NACSCORP
Espresso Book Machine

For Lightning UK:
Amazon.co.uk
Bertrams
Blackwell
Book Depository
Coutts
Gardners
Mallory International
Eden Interactive Ltd.
Aphrohead

Paperback Bookshop (parent of Books2Anywhere)
Biblica UK (formerly IBS-STL UK, parent of STL Distribution)
Argosy (Ireland)
Libreria Ledi (Italy)
Eleftheroudakis (Greece)
Agapea (Spain)

Get the Connection

Though Lightning Source is now becoming better-known among self publishers, for many years there were few who had heard of it at all. And there was a good reason for that. Lightning prefers to deal with publishers and self publishing companies rather than with authors directly. That minimizes Lightning's need to provide customer support.

But then, how can you work with Lightning directly? Simple. You become a publisher. And thankfully, Lightning makes that step easier than ever before. Though there are a number of things you might need or want to do in setting up a publishing business, only two are vital for working with Lightning: adopting a publishing name and acquiring a set of ISBNs—International Standard Book Numbers. (I'll discuss all this later, in detail.)

Even if you live outside the U.S. or U.K., you're not left out. Because of the Internet, you can work directly either with Lightning US or with Lightning UK from anywhere in the world. In fact, Lightning UK is set up to do business not only in English but also in French, German, Spanish, and Italian. And the books Lightning prints can be in any language at all!

Before you read any further, though, I must caution you that working with Lightning is not the best choice, or even a good one, for most self publishers. This route will suit you only if you're:

- Planning to publish more than one book. The setup and learning probably won't be worth it for just one or two.
- Profit-oriented. Willing to make the extra effort to earn a good return on your investment.
- A good marketer. You won't make money if you're not willing and able to promote your book, at least at the start.

• Financially able. It takes money to make money, and you'll have to be ready to plunk down cash when needed (though what's needed can be much, much less than with self publishing companies or old-style self publishing).

• Possessing a good business attitude. That means being able to work with others in the industry professionally and courteously, without undue suspiciousness or an attitude of "us against them."

• Technically capable. Able to work with computers effectively and to understand complex instructions. With minimal help from Lightning itself, you'll need to perform a variety of demanding tasks in complicated software and on arcane Web sites—or else engage others to handle them for you.*

I can't stress this last point enough. If you're the kind of person who often gets stuck on the computer and needs to be bailed out by others, do yourself a favor and either farm out the work or stay away from Lightning Source! Lightning is set up to work with professionals who don't need such help, and you simply won't get it.

---

* To find consultants who can help you, see the "Other Resources" listings on my Publishing Page. And no, I don't offer such services myself!

Get the Advantage

The demands of working with Lightning Source are great, but so can be the rewards. By cutting out the self publishing companies that act as middlemen and then working directly with Lightning, you can as much as double your profit per copy. That's because you don't have that intermediary applying a markup to printing costs or taking a big cut of the book's income.

But how does this arrangement compare financially to old-style self publishing—printing large numbers of copies, then marketing through traditional bookselling channels? Isn't printing on demand much more expensive than the offset printing used for large press runs, making it harder to turn a profit with POD?

Yes and no. Yes, direct printing costs per copy are higher, but this is most often balanced by costs you avoid. You don't pay for shipping, you don't pay for copies you wind up not selling, you don't miss sales if you run out of stock at a bad time. In the end, it's likely to even out, or even come out in favor of going with Lightning.

But more importantly, when you work directly with Lightning, the ways to increase profit per copy are no longer limited to cutting your costs or raising your price. In fact, you can double the profit without touching those factors at all—because for the first time, you have real control over discount.

Let me explain. It seems that in field after field of creative or productive endeavor, the people in the middle claim all the power and call all the shots. The actual creator or producer most often winds up having to accept whatever's offered and then barely scraping by on it—or not. And the smaller you are, the more you're at their mercy.

This is certainly true in publishing. When small publishers are allowed into regular book channels at all, their benefactors often charge them a larger-than-standard cut for the privilege.

Amazon does this with its Advantage program for buying books directly from small publishers—the advantage of the program being Amazon's, not the publisher's. Ingram does it with its on-again off-again small publisher program. But even Ingram's regular publishers are required to give Ingram a discount of over half the cover price of the book. And what of the publishers Ingram says are too small to work with directly? In the past, their only course was to go through a distributor that charged them a hefty percentage over Ingram's.

Lightning Source, though, was set up to be different. Part of its aim was to attract academic and library publishers who never offer a wholesaler the kinds of discounts that Ingram normally requires for stocking. So, Ingram wound up creating a back door to its operation—an entry point that doesn't require publishers to follow Ingram's normal rules. Small publishers working with Lightning are allowed to set *almost any discount to wholesalers that they want!*

I'll come back to the whole question of setting your Lightning discount to maximize profit. But for now, here are some other great benefits of working with Lightning:

• Unlike if you were supplying Ingram or Baker & Taylor directly, you can choose not to allow booksellers to return copies of your book, eliminating that notorious source of hassle, cost, and waste.

• You don't have to invoice (as with old-style self publishing) or wonder about what's owed to you (as when working with some self publishing companies). Lightning keeps track of everything, provides detailed sales reports, and sends payment reliably each month.

• With its history of profitability and stability, you don't have to worry about Lightning closing its doors or being absorbed into another company, as you might with a self publishing company or a small press distributor.

• Your agreement with Lightning is nonexclusive. That means, if you have a different, better way to supply special markets, you can pursue that too.

Quite simply, for any self publisher able to handle the challenges, there's no better deal in print publishing.

Get Access

Lightning Source—for the U.S., the U.K., or anywhere else—can be found at

www.lightningsource.com

For introductory info in French, German, Spanish, or Italian, or for the U.K., choose from the "International Sites" menu. Email addresses include

Inquiry@lightningsource.com
Enquiries@lightningsource.co.uk
SalesQuotes@lightningsource.com
NewAccounts@lightningsource.com

The Espresso Book Machine

The Espresso has generated a lot of hoopla—from one standpoint, probably more than it deserves. Many small publishers see it as a promising new way to reach into the stores that now ignore them. But it isn't. All Lightning Source books are already available to customers of those stores through special order. Ordering a book on the Espresso is not really different in kind from ordering it for printing and delivery in a few days. Yes, it's quicker, but speed isn't your main obstacle to sales.

In each case—instant printing or printing in a big distribution center—the problem for the small publisher is how to make your books *known*. The Espresso won't help with that. Just as before, the best bet for small publishers will be to aim at *online* booksellers, where your books *can* be made easy to discover. (This is not even to mention that there are expected to be only eighty of these machines in the entire world by the end of 2011.)

Then where lies the importance of the Espresso for the small publisher? I believe it is in international markets. Clearly, Lightning has been slower in expanding overseas than previously hoped. The expense and complexity of building a large POD operation is a huge deterrent, as is the problem of adapting to a foreign language and business culture.

But what if you have a (relatively) small machine available to regional distributors and retailers in a given country, and economical for even a small market? You would then find your books selling competitively in that country through its Internet booksellers, effectively expanding your market with no direct investment or adaptation at all.

So, don't expect the Espresso Book Machine to do a lot for your books in the U.S., Canada, or the U.K. But look for it to open up Australia, New Zealand, and South Africa, among others. Yes, Lightning books are already available online in these countries—but the Espresso will let your books be sold there faster and cheaper, thereby increasing demand.

Already, Angus & Robertson, Australia's largest bookstore chain and a major online bookseller, has begun deploying fifty of the machines. Don't be surprised by a 5% to 10% boost in sales over time, just from international markets and the Espresso.

2
Becoming a Publisher

Adopt a Name

When does an author become a publisher? When they take control of the entire process of producing a book and getting it to market. That doesn't mean you have to do everything yourself. But even when you engage others to help you, you're in charge of each step.

To a large extent, it's a matter of mindset. If you think you're a publisher, and you act like a publisher—you're a publisher! And a very important part of that is adopting a publishing name.

Your publishing name is what you call your publishing business or company—even if that "company" is no one but you. Though it's technically possible to do without such a name—even when working with Lightning Source—you and your book will get a lot less respect if the publisher is listed only as "Arthur Author." (Or more likely, "Author, Arthur.") In fact, using your personal name could well be a flag that makes Lightning think twice about working with you at all. Besides, having a spiffy publishing name is just more fun!

A good publishing name matches the tone and content of the books that will be published under it. You don't want to publish *Logarithmic Statistics for the Corporate Engineer* under Floppy Dog Books. Or *I Just Love You SO Much* under Quantum Technologies Press. But also choose a name you can grow into, not one limited to your first book or your current situation. (I'm sure self-publishing guru Dan Poynter regrets "Para Publishing," chosen because his first book was about parachuting.)

If you plan to publish widely different types of books, you might also consider creating names for one or more *imprints*—kind of like company divisions, except you don't have to walk down a hall to get to them. For instance, I now publish all my nonfiction under my company name, Shepard Publications, but I publish children's books under the imprint Skyhook Press, while my wife, Anne's, novels come out under Shepard & Piper. I also shepherded in my older publishing company, Simple Productions, making it an imprint of the new one. (Yes, that was a pun.)

You might also create an imprint if you're publishing under an existing company with an unsuitable name. For instance, a book buyer might be cautious about a book published by Acme Sanitation but not think twice about one from its imprint, Trash Press. Or you might want to mask your company's association with a book, as might the Freedom Rifle Company if it ever published *A Handbook for Gun Control Activists.*

As I'll discuss along the way, Lightning and the other businesses and services you'll work with all accommodate imprint names. Be aware, though, that adding each imprint takes some effort and brings a new level of complexity to your operation. If you can possibly stick to one publishing name, I advise you to do it.

By the way, another use of the word *imprint* is *any* name under which you publish, including your primary publishing name. So, don't get confused if you see it used that way.

Before settling on a publishing or imprint name, make sure it's not already in use in the publishing world or on the Web. To check in publishing, search for the name on Amazon with its Advanced Search for Books.

www.amazon.com/exec/obidos/ats-query-page

To check the Web, type "www.publishingname.com"—no, not literally, you have to replace the middle part—into your browser. (Though you could check it on a domain registration site, that's generally not a good idea at first, since a scalper may then register the name if you delay doing it yourself.)

With the huge number of people now publishing, and the even greater number of people creating Web sites, finding a unique and amenable name becomes harder and harder. With a domain name, you might get around that with different punctuation or spelling or an extension other than ".com"—but I don't advise it, because it will make you harder to find.

Unusual combinations of words are one way to deal with the problem. At this writing, "Omnipotent Slug Books" and "Lazy Dynamo Press" are both available. Local place names are another possibility.

But whatever name you want and determine is available, register the domain name as soon as you're sure, to keep anyone else from grabbing it. You don't need to wait till you're ready to put up a site or even till you know what company will host it. Though it's common for Web hosts to offer domain name registration, you can get it separately instead. (In fact, that's better, because you don't want to switch registrars if you change hosts.)*

You don't plan to put up a Web site at all? Register the name anyway. You might change your mind later. And even if you don't, you want to keep anyone else from putting up a site that could be mistaken as yours.

---

* My own favored domain name registrar is Network Solutions. It's not the cheapest, but it was originally the sole registrar for the U.S. and is about as established and reliable as you can get. I take no chances with domain names.

Obtain ISBNs

ISBN stands for *International Standard Book Number.* (Please don't say "ISBN number." It's redundant.) The ISBN is what's used in the book trade to identify each published book in each edition and format, along with the company that has published it. In the publishing world, owning your own ISBNs is the most important thing that defines you as a publisher. *It is also Lightning's one absolute requirement for distributing your books.*

The ISBN is used most prominently in the bar code on the back of a book, being encoded in the bars themselves and also printed above them. For this reason, beginning self publishers often make the mistake of thinking the ISBN *is* the bar code and that obtaining a bar code will automatically give them an ISBN—or vice versa. An ISBN, though, is just a number, while a bar code is just a way to represent a number graphically. So, you need to obtain the ISBN *before* you can put it in a bar code.

Though the ISBN of your book can be used in selling it anywhere in the world, that number must still be obtained in your own country or region. Each such country or region has its own agency for selling or granting ISBNs. This agency might be run by the government, or by an industry group, or by a private company.

The U.S. ISBN Agency is run by R. R. Bowker, a private company, which sells ISBNs through a site called Identifier Services.* Find it at

www.myidentifiers.com

---

* Bowker's older site for selling ISBNs is www.isbn.org. At this writing, that site is slated to be closed down "soon."

The U.K. agency is run by Nielsen BookData.

www.isbn.nielsenbookdata.co.uk

And here are addresses for the ISBN agencies of several other countries, for those living in them.

> **www.collectionscanada.gc.ca/isn** (Canada)
> **www.thorpe.com.au/isbn** (Australia)
> **www.natlib.govt.nz/services/**
> **get-advice/publishing/isbn** (New Zealand)

For any other country, do an Internet search on "ISBN" plus the country name, or visit the International ISBN Agency at

www.isbn-international.org

Of course, you'll want to apply for ISBNs under your publishing name—so that needs to be squared away first.

ISBNs are normally acquired in a "block" of 10 or 100 or even more. The prices of ISBNs range from expensive (U.S.) to free (Canada). A block of ten U.S. ISBNs will at this writing cost $250—which is certainly a lot if you might not be using many of them, but perhaps still not a huge price for admission to the publishing world.

Within each block of 10 or 100 numbers, the only digits that vary from one number to the next are the last two or three. The digits that stay the same constitute a *publisher prefix* and are what identify you as the publisher. For instance, in the ISBN for *POD for Profit,* 978-0-938497-46-2, the publisher prefix is 978-0-938497, and that's the same for all books I publish.

If you use up your set, you can buy additional blocks, but each will have a different prefix, which can complicate your listings. So, if you can afford it, it's best to start with as large a block as you'll ever likely need. The supply of ISBNs, though, is not infinite even if huge, and your country's ISBN agency, after considering your publishing plans, may limit the size of the block you can acquire. (And even if it dispenses ISBNs freely and without limit, please be considerate and take no more than a reasonable number.)

If you're publishing under different imprints, you might want to obtain a different set of ISBNs for each, to help keep them straight. But that's not required. The ISBNs belong to your publishing company and can be allocated as you wish.

It's now possible to obtain a single, standalone ISBN in the U.S. and some other countries (but not presently in the U.K.). But unless you're really sure you'll never publish another book, buying a single ISBN is not a good idea. The problem is that you'll be sharing a publisher prefix with all other purchasers of single ISBNs in your country or region. (In the U.S., this prefix is 978-0-6151.) This may cause confusion and complication down the line when your prefix is expected to identify you, and it might bar you from some listing agencies. Also, at this writing, the cost in the U.S. of a single ISBN is half the cost of ten—so it's a pretty poor deal.

Note that if you're reissuing a book that you first brought out through a self publishing company, you *cannot* reuse the old ISBN. That number identifies the self publishing company as the publisher, so you *must* replace it with one of your own.* Likewise, do not fall for any offers of low-cost ISBNs from a source other than your region's official ISBN agency. If you pay

---

* As an exception, about a dozen U.S. self publishing companies optionally offer single ISBNs from Bowker that you can keep using when you leave the company—including Lulu.com. But since Lightning prints and distributes for Lulu and most other such companies and doesn't want to be seen as stealing their customers, it's doubtful you could reuse one there.

less than the official price, then you are only buying limited use of someone else's ISBN.

If you purchase ISBNs from Bowker, you may be presented with additional offers and opportunities, and you might wonder if you need them. These may include:

• SAN (Standard Address Number). This helps some retail booksellers automate their direct orders to publishers. It is not likely to be useful to you.

• DOI (Digital Object Identifier). This can identify a work in all its physical and digital formats—useful especially when there are too many formats to assign ISBNs economically—and also serves as a pointer to book info hosted online. But so far, the DOI hasn't caught on, so it's not likely to help you.

• Bar codes with your ISBNs embedded. You don't need to buy these, because Lightning supplies them for free. (That is, the *bar codes* are free, not the ISBNs.)

My advice: Just take the ISBNs and run.*

If you're applying for ISBNs from Nielsen BookData for the first time, you may run into a proverbial chicken-and-egg situation: They'll want you to supply details on your book, and even copies of the title page and title verso, long before you're likely to be prepared for that.

Your best bet is to construct dummy versions of the pages Nielsen requests and just guess at any book info yet to be determined. You can change that info later through Nielsen's PubWeb, which I'll discuss shortly.

Note that *not* all fields in the Nielsen ISBN application are mandatory. Also, you can omit the distributor name for now, though it will be Lightning Source UK once you've signed up there.

---

* On Bowker's old isbn.org site, you're also offered a paid subscription to an ISBN Online Logbook—another offer you can safely pass up.

Set Up for Business

In establishing a business, there are a number of other things you may want or need to deal with, whether or not Lightning Source requires them. First let's look at a few legal and financial matters.

Note that these items are based on the simplest form of business, commonly called *sole proprietor* or *sole trader*. Incorporation or other structured legal forms of organization might have advantages in some cases—for instance, when there's a high risk of legal liability—but they are not normally necessary to becoming a self publisher. Also note, if you already have a business of some kind, much of this might piggyback on your current setup.

• Business name registration. Local law may require this *if* you're doing business *locally* under your publishing name. In the U.S., this is usually done through the county clerk. What you're registering will be called something like *fictitious business name,* DBA ("doing business as"), or TA ("trading as").*

• Business bank account in your publishing name. You'll need your business name registration to get one of these. The account will allow you to write and accept checks in that name. But you probably don't need a business account for the sake of Lightning, because you can arrange for direct electronic deposit into any U.S., U.K., or E.U. account, and you can write checks to Lightning under any name—and anyway, you can make payments by credit card instead.

• State or provincial sales tax license, certificate, or permit (or VAT or GST license, in some countries). This one *can* be a hassle, because with one of these, you'll be required to report

---

* *Fictitious* here does *not* mean "fraudulent." There's nothing illegal or unethical about using a business name.

and pay at least yearly, and possibly more often. But a sales tax license—unlike one for VAT or GST—is needed *only* if you sell direct to the public, *not* when you sell to distributors, wholesalers, bookstores, or other retailers. So, to avoid this hassle, you can simply decide not to sell to the public. (Lightning may *ask* for your sales tax license number but will not *require* you to provide one.)

• Business taxes. If you're a publisher, you are self-employed. That means, if you make any significant amount of money, your taxes will become more complex and will be more fully your responsibility. (In the U.S., Lightning issues 1099 income reports for sole proprietors.)

By the way, when dealing with business legalities and taxes, your only concerns are with the country you're living in. You don't need to worry about other countries where Lightning might be selling your books.

Another part of being a publisher is simply looking the part. Here are a few props I strongly recommend.

• Web site. Nowadays, everyone expects to be able to find you on the Web. Of course, a Web site can be a tremendous sales tool for your books—but at the least, you want it to provide basic info on your company, plus one or more ways to contact you. As an example, here's the "publisher" site I maintain separately from my much more elaborate "author" sites.

www.shepardpub.com

• Business email address. You'll find that something like YourName@yourcompany.com is most respectable, but even YourCompany@yourISP.com will do in a pinch. Nowadays, Gmail addresses are also OK. Just don't figure on getting much respect with an address from Hotmail or Yahoo!

• Stationery with your publishing name—letterhead, envelope, mailing labels. Nowadays, this is only for occasional use. Don't get anything printed commercially or spend any money on this, just whip it up in your computer. For instance, for my letterhead, I have a custom Microsoft Word template with my publishing name, address, and phone number in the header, and my email and Web addresses in the footer. I type into the body of the document, then print out everything together. My envelopes and mailing labels are printed out ahead and hand addressed. Mailing labels are printed out a sheet at a time from a file formatted with a table.

A final part of becoming a publisher is equipping yourself properly for the work. Though you can self publish on a shoestring, or farm out work to skilled professionals, the right paraphernalia can make it much easier and more enjoyable to perform any tasks you take on. Here's what I recommend for the complete do-it-yourselfer.

• Good computer. A computer of some kind is a must, of course. A good one is highly desirable, if you can manage it. Especially if you're working with graphics, this can save you a lot of frustration.

• Broadband Internet access. Lightning actually mentions this on its site as a requirement, though that's probably an overstatement. Anyway, with the size of files you're likely to send and receive, and the slowness of many publishing Web sites, this should be near the top of your wish list.

• Laser printer. Though such printers are more expensive than inkjets to buy, they save you much money in the long run by their cheaper operating cost. Also, they run much faster, and their output is much more professional.

• Inkjet printer. Unless you have a color laser printer, you'll want one of these too if you're designing your own covers or doing anything else in color.

• Scanner. You're likely to find many, many uses for this. For myself, I'm thoroughly dependent on my tabloid ("large format") scanner.

• Publishing software. You can compose a simple book in a word processor like Microsoft Word, and graphics can be handled in an inexpensive graphics program like Adobe Photoshop Elements. For working with Lightning, though, I strongly recommend also getting a copy of Adobe Acrobat, preferably in the Pro version. (I'll tell you later how to buy it for less.) For designing covers, or books with many graphics, a page layout program like Adobe InDesign is worth the investment, if you can afford the price and the learning time.

Does the process and cost of becoming a publisher seem intimidating? Well, it's certainly no stroll in the park. But as I said, most of this is not required just to work with Lightning. And much of the rest, if you need or want it, can be added as you go along.

Real Self Publishing?

In my books, I refer to providers of POD author services by the common term "self publishing company." Many Old Guard self publishers object to this term, saying customers of these companies are not really self publishing at all, and insisting the companies be called vanity publishers or subsidy publishers instead. They also point out that a self publishing *company* is a contradiction in terms.

But this is just playing Humpty Dumpty with the language. A self publisher is anyone who pays the money and makes the decisions—and that *does* include customers of these companies. What's more, any company that helps self publishers has every right to call itself a "self publishing company." After all, we have self publishing *books* and self publishing *consultants*. Why not self publishing *companies*?

Vanity publishing is itself a *subset* of self publishing, and always has been. *Subsidy publishing,* on the other hand, means that the author and the publisher *share* the cost and control. Since these modern companies invest nothing of their own in the books' success, they are definitely *not* subsidy publishers!

And how do I distinguish a customer of such a company from someone like myself, with my own business setup, ISBNs, and so on? Certainly not by calling myself a "real" self publisher! My choice of terms is *independent self publisher*. But that's only a term of convenience, not status, and *any* self publisher should be proud to be one.

Plug Into Lightning

As soon as you have your publishing name and ISBNs, you're ready for an account at Lightning Source. And you'll need the account well before your book is ready for design and production, so you can get full access to documentation.

Here again is where to find Lightning for both the U.S. and U.K. branches.

www.lightningsource.com

Opening an account starts with filling out the application for new customers on Lightning's Web site. Click the "Register" button on the home page, then the link for publishers. You'll be asked for contact info, plus info on your publishing operation and plans. The latter will help Lightning determine whether you're ready to work with them or might better be referred to a self publishing company. If there's any question about it, you should receive a phone call to discuss it.

But don't get too nervous. At this writing, I don't know of any self publisher who has been turned down—except one unfortunate woman who declined to provide a phone number! Still, you want to seem as professional as possible. Among other things, that means applying with your publishing name instead of a personal one.

Your own title in the "company"? "President," "owner," or "publisher" will do. For "Form of Business," say "Sole Proprietor," unless you're sure you're something else.

"Total number of titles in print" refers to books for which *you* are the publisher. Don't count any book of yours that came out under another publisher's name.

Be careful with one question: "Will you need assistance with editing, book design, or cover layout?" This really means,

"Will you need such assistance *from Lightning Source?*" If you need help but plan to get it elsewhere, then the appropriate answer here is no. If you do hope to get it from Lightning—well then, you're in the wrong place entirely, and you can expect to be told so!

The response to your online application may be an email with another set of questions. The only question that might be tricky is, "Have your titles been printed/published by any company other than your own? If so, by whom?"—referring to titles you're planning to send to Lightning.

Lightning asks this because it wants to make sure it's not stealing business from any of its clients, which in North America include just about every single self publishing company. So, for any book you intend to move to Lightning from such a company, plan to issue it in a new edition with a new ISBN—even if you own the old ISBN and don't intend to change a thing in the book. Since a new edition is considered a "new title," that will allow you to honestly answer no to Lightning's question.

In the same vein, you don't want to otherwise volunteer the info that you've worked with a self publishing company. One publisher did so *after* approval and was told by Lightning UK that, if they'd known he was a Lulu customer at all, they would not have opened his account!

For more details on moving to Lightning from a self publishing company, see the special section "Moving to Lightning" later in this book.

Once your application is approved, you'll receive a home account at either Lightning US or Lightning UK, depending on your country. The world outside the U.S. and the U.K. is divvied up between the two, with all publishers in the European Union, for instance, going to Lightning UK. You cannot choose which Lightning you're assigned to or request to be switched.

You may be asked for up to three of your ISBN publisher prefixes. As I explained earlier, you find the prefix by seeing which digits in a set of ISBNs stay the same for each number—generally, all but the last two or three digits. Unless you've bought more than one set, you'll have only one prefix. If you have only a single ISBN, leave this blank and explain that later.

You'll also be asked to fill out various forms and agreements according to which services you want Lightning to provide. Basically, you should opt for *all* services related to print on demand. (eBook services will be offered too, but the current ones are not very useful, and you can always add them later.)

Services offered by Lightning will include:

Publisher Direct Order Service. This allows you to order copies of your own book, for shipment either to yourself or to any other address of your choice. It's the most basic level of service when you apply for an account. When you order books in this way, you're really just using Lightning as a printer—more specifically, a "short run" printer, meaning a printer handling orders smaller than the book industry norm. You can set this up for printing by Lightning US and/or Lightning UK.

Direct ordering provides you with a basic form of *drop shipping*—sending books directly to customers as if they came from you. Though a bit awkward and expensive for sending single copies to individual purchasers, this system works well for occasional shipments to booksellers.

Note, though, that when *Lightning* says "drop shipping," it's talking about a different service entirely, involving a sophisticated system called EDI (Electronic Data Interchange) that no self publisher is likely to need. So, if you come across what *Lightning* describes as instructions for drop shipping, just ignore them.

Wholesale Order Service. With this additional service, Lightning distributes your book, selling it to Ingram, Amazon, and other wholesalers and retailers. It's the main reason you're signing up with Lightning! This service too can be arranged from Lightning US and/or Lightning UK. Also, you can sign up for direct distribution to Canada and the European Union in their native currencies—though at this writing, these "channels" have not been activated.

Important: *To get wholesale order services from both Lightning US and Lightning UK, you must sign a separate agreement for each.* For Canadian and E.U. distribution, you must sign "amendments." (If you're an older customer who wants to add distribution options, see the special section "Adding Distribution Options" later in this book.)

You'll also be offered an agreement for distribution through the Espresso Book Machine. This can include distribution to any number of countries, though you'll need to "turn them on" individually as the Espresso finds its way to new ones.

Not sure you need all those services? Don't worry. Doing the paperwork now doesn't obligate you to use them all for any book. It just means they'll be available if you want them.

Note that Lightning's main U.S. and U.K. agreements both have a fill-in blank for where you're incorporated. This is *not* a sneaky way to slip in a requirement for incorporation, it's simply a vestige of a time when Lightning was dealing almost entirely with corporations. Just write in "U.S.," "U.K.," or whatever other country you live in.

Your profit from book sales comes to you from Lightning US and/or Lightning UK once a month in the currency of your primary account—either U.S. dollars, British pounds, or euros, depending on where you live. You can get each of those two payments by check, but it's quicker and simpler if you can receive them as deposits directly into your bank account. This service is available to customers with bank accounts in the U.S., the U.K., or the E.U., and you'll be asked for the required bank info as you set up your Lightning account.

If you do *not* have a bank account in any of these countries, you'll probably have to stick with receiving checks. In some cases, it's possible to get a bank account in a country without living there—for instance, if you register a business there—but most of the time, it won't be worth the hassle.*

To get you set up for your own direct ordering, Lightning will ask for either a credit card or business references for trade credit. Generally, it's simplest to supply a credit card, which can then also be used to pay Lightning's book setup and maintenance fees. Charges from Lightning US will always be in dollars, and those from Lightning UK will always be in pounds or euros—but most credit cards will handle any needed conversion automatically.

If you're in the U.S., Lightning may ask questions to determine whether you should be paying sales tax on your book orders. The correct answer is to claim exemption because any books you order will be for resale, not personal use.

You may then be asked to fill out a form to declare your compliance with your state's sales tax law. This form will ask for your sales tax license number. Remember, you are *not* legally required to have such a license unless you plan to sell directly to the public. If you don't have one and don't need one, just leave this blank. Your Lightning application does not hinge on your providing one, and Lightning isn't set up to collect sales tax anyway—it just wants to be able to say it isn't knowingly breaking any sales tax law itself.

---

* One exception may be for Canadians, who can sign up for a true U.S. bank account through Royal Bank of Canada—though the account is reportedly subject to large fees.

Also if you're in the U.S., you may be asked to fill out a W-9 form for federal taxpayer identification. To claim exemption from backup withholding, check "Exempt payee."

If you want to publish books under an imprint—a publishing name other than your main one—Lightning will need to set up that name in the system before the books are submitted.

Request Listings

Whether or not your marketing is focused on Amazon, you want reliable data on your book to be available wherever booksellers and book buyers might look for it. You also want one or more authoritative sources where you can park any book data differing from what's at Lightning—for instance, a subtitle that's longer than Lightning and Ingram can accommodate, or one you've altered since publication without wanting to deal with Lightning's problematic process for metadata changes.

To handle all this, you want to work with the two most important independent book listing businesses: R. R. Bowker in the U.S. and Nielsen BookData in the U.K.—yes, the same companies that sell ISBNs in those countries.

R. R. Bowker issues Books in Print plus other authoritative online databases. Though once the unrivalled reference to available books for U.S. booksellers and librarians, Books in Print now competes for that role with the catalogs of Ingram, Baker & Taylor, and Amazon.com. But it still reportedly serves over three thousand clients, including Barnes & Noble, Borders, nearly two thousand libraries and library systems, and a number of school systems and smaller retailers. Amazon itself, in its early years, drew data extensively from Books in Print but no longer uses it in any way.

Let me repeat that, because the opposing claim arises wherever two or more self publishers are gathered together: *Amazon no longer receives any data from Bowker's Books in Print.*

There's no charge to list books in Books in Print, and any publisher—including those outside the U.S.—can do that. If you bought your ISBNs through Bowker's Identifier Services, you already have a "My Identifiers" account that lets you submit book info through that site. Again, that's at

www.myidentifiers.com

The word from Bowker is that *all* online submissions to Books in Print will eventually go through My Identifiers accounts. But for now, if you did *not* get your ISBNs through Identifier Services, it might be best to use Bowker's older publisher portal, BowkerLink. For info on that, see "Working with BowkerLink" in the appendix.

With a My Identifiers account, you'll need to have Bowker add distributor names to it, and also imprint names, if you have any. Email these, along with your ISBN prefix, to Bowker's Publishers Authority Database department, at

PAD@bowker.com

The distributor names should be "Lightning Source, Incorporated" and "Lightning Source UK Limited." *Do not try to add Ingram.* That's a wholesaler, not a distributor, and will not be accepted.

Some self publishers might be tempted not to offer the distributor info, in an attempt to escape a supposed stigma of print on demand. But this is not the place to do that. Books in Print is used largely to locate books for special orders, and listing Lightning Source will tell most Bowker users that your books can be obtained from major wholesalers. If you leave that out, the person ordering may try to order from you direct— and probably one of the last things you want is to fill orders for one or two copies.

While Bowker's Books in Print has waned in importance, Nielsen BookData has remained dominant in the U.K., and also in supplying data on British books to other countries—110 of them, according to Nielsen. Its data is used by the major U.K. wholesalers and chains and by Amazon sites outside the U.S. So, having an accurate listing there can be greatly important. I suggest you set up an account *at least* one month before you plan to launch your book—two months for safety.

Nielsen's publisher interface is called PubWeb. You can find the service and download an application at

www.nielsenbookdata.com/pubweb

To download the application, click on "Not a registered user?" (Don't get confused by any "Register" button for BookNet Web or BookData Online, which are different Nielsen services.)

List your distributor as Lightning Source UK. For some reason, Nielsen may then change this to either Bertrams or Gardners, the two largest U.K. wholesalers handling books from Lightning UK—but at least you'll know you tried to supply accurate info. As with Bowker, you can instead leave this blank, but this may cause some booksellers to try to order direct.

If you got your ISBNs from Nielsen, there should be no question about your getting an account. But otherwise, Nielsen may contact you to say they have no record of any of your books, or that Lightning UK will take care of your listings. In such a case, tell them that you have a book coming and you want to submit the listing yourself so that you can control its content.

Nielsen may also offer to "split" your listings between you and Lightning UK. Under this arrangement, Nielsen would rely on Lightning for "trade data"—price, availability, and publication date—while you would supply all supplementary info yourself. This isn't a bad idea—but since I haven't tried it myself, I can't say how well it might work in practice!

A basic account with PubWeb is free, but it now has premium, paid accounts for enhanced listings. This might be worthwhile for some publishers, but it's not necessary just for selling on Amazon, because you can always give additional material to Amazon directly.

PubWeb will let you view your publisher info via links from your book listings, but you will not be able to edit it online. If you're in the U.S., the contact info is not likely to bring you direct orders, but if you're in the U.K., you might want to try to get it removed. Do this by writing to

PubHelp.Book@nielsen.com

For PubWeb too, additional imprint names must be submitted ahead of time by email.

Nielsen is notoriously difficult to work with, and you may find yourself wondering if it's worth the effort. And actually, if you don't supply your book's data to Nielsen, then Lightning UK will do it for you. But then Lightning will "own" that listing, and you won't be able to change or add to it without getting the "ownership" transferred to you. Your best bet, then, is to set up with Nielsen right at the start to avoid such complications.

Access Wholesalers

Lightning Source will distribute your book to the top book wholesalers of both the U.S. and the U.K. This means you do *not* have to sign up with wholesalers to directly supply books yourself. And you shouldn't! Supplying direct would mean giving up control of your discount and other terms, as well as dealing with businesses known for poor treatment of small publishers.

But because of their importance in the supply chain, you do want to take advantage of any opportunities to access your book info at these wholesalers. Such access is made available in different degrees by both of the top two in the U.S.—Ingram Book Company and Baker & Taylor.

The most important wholesaler for you to access will be Ingram, because of its close relationships with both Lightning and Amazon.com. Being a Lightning publisher entitles you to a free account on ipage, Ingram's Web portal, found at

ipage.ingrambook.com

To get an ipage account, just ask Lightning to have one set up for you. That will let you check your book's listing, status, and stocking at Ingram.*

Your ipage account will be essential in following the progress of your book's setup, and also in tracking down the source of problems that might show up on Amazon and other online booksellers. Ninety percent of the time, trouble with a book's availability or listing on Amazon is due to Ingram—but if you

---

* FREDDIE, Ingram's automated phone-in service for book info for publishers, has been discontinued.

can't check your book on ipage, you'll be flying blind, not sure who to blame.

Technically, the kind of ipage account that Lightning will give you is a *bookseller* or *retailer* account—though you won't be able to buy books with it. Publishers who have been with Lightning since before this was offered may have applied directly to ipage and received a *publisher* or *supplier* account—but this is no longer available to new Lightning publishers.* (For more on publisher accounts, see "iPage Publisher Accounts" in the appendix.)

Not sure which kind of ipage account you have? Look at the tabs. The tabs for a bookseller account are "Browse & Search," "Merch & Promotions," "Order," "Account Mgmt.," "Reports," and "Programs & Catalogs." The tabs for a publisher account are "Browse & Search," "Purchase Orders," "Reports," "Information Mgmt.," and "Marketing & Promotions."

Baker & Taylor, unlike Ingram, doesn't give Lightning publishers free access to its catalog—but if you're feeling flush, it does offer *paid* access through a service called Publisher Alley. That's at

www.puballey.com

The info available through this service can help you track down sticky problems with listings, availability, and price, on Amazon as well as elsewhere on the Web. You'll also get access to your book's sales history at B&T.

Publisher Alley is available by yearly subscriptions that are expensive, as well as a hassle to set up. (You actually have to sign a paper contract sent by postal mail—every year!) You'll have to decide for yourself if it's worth it. But if you don't want

---

* Actually, you can *still* get a publisher account directly from ipage, but it won't be associated with your Lightning books—so it's not much use.

to pay up and don't need access for long, you can get a free trial—which would probably be enough to deal with a single book. In either case, you might wait to apply till your book is almost ready for sale, so you're not paying for access you don't yet need.

Stake Your Claims

Self publishers may stew at the idea of people photocopying portions of their books instead of buying them. But believe it or not, you can make money off that. And depending on where you live, you might also make money if someone borrows your book from a library.

In the U.S., it's illegal to photocopy substantial portions of a copyrighted work without the rights holder's permission. In many other countries, though, it's legal as long as the person or organization copying the material pays a fee. This fee is collected by a national *reproduction rights organization* (RRO) and distributed as royalties to rights holders within that country. Or for foreign works, the fee is sent to the RRO of the other country to be distributed there. In this way, royalties from overseas are paid even to U.S. right holders, though no such fees are collected in the U.S.

You can receive these royalties not only for your books but for anything of yours that might be photocopied, including materials on your Web site or blog. All you must do is make sure the work that's copied can be associated with you and that everyone knows where to send the money. And part of doing that is to sign up with your own RRO.

In the U.S., the RRO is Copyright Clearance Center (CCC), and you sign up at Rights Central.

rightscentral.copyright.com

Sign up under your *personal* name, with your publishing name for "Organization." Watch out for the phone number format.

Have you already had a payment from CCC? Then you already have an account there, and signing up at Rights Central will let you access it. On the form, avoid confusion by supplying the account number, which CCC can give you on request if you don't know it. You may even have more than one existing account. Before I ever signed up, CCC had opened accounts for both Aaron Shepard and Shepard Publications.

CCC offers a variety of tools for managing rights sales—not only for books but for all your public content, including Web pages. You may or may not find those tools useful, and you're free to ignore them. The most important thing is to keep the agency supplied with current contact info—and bank info too, if you opt for direct deposit. To help CCC along in figuring who gets money, you may also want to register your books as they're published—especially if they're from more than one author or under more than one imprint.

Is signing up worth it? It *can* be, especially if you've published anything likely to be photocopied in bulk. For instance, I've published several books with reader's theater materials, primarily for classroom use, with more on my Web site. Out of the blue, I've received several payments from CCC for overseas copying of these materials, for a total of several thousand dollars—even though my books and Web site clearly state that the materials may be copied at no charge.

But even if you're not expecting big payments, it's probably worth enrolling in CCC just to avoid potential messes. I learned this lesson the hard way when a royalty check of theirs for close to a thousand dollars took several months to be forwarded from a previous address of mine. This payment had been reported by CCC to the government as taxable income—but because of its delay in reaching me, I knew nothing about it till *after* the deadline for tax reporting!

As I said, each country has its own reproduction rights organization. If you're in the U.K., enroll in the Authors' Licensing and Collecting Society (ALCS) *and* the Publishers Licensing Society (PLS).

www.alcs.co.uk
www.pls.org.uk

In Canada, it's Access Copyright.

www.accesscopyright.ca

In Australia, you want Copyright Agency Limited (CAL).

www.copyright.com.au

And in New Zealand, Copyright Licensing Ltd. (CLL).

www.copyright.co.nz

To find out about agencies in other countries, visit the International Federation of Reproduction Rights Organisations (IFRRO).

www.ifrro.org

Many countries—though not the U.S.—also have arrangements to collect and distribute fees for books owned or loaned by libraries. The terms that refer to this are "public lending right" and "educational lending right," for public and educational libraries respectively. Sign up with one of these registration agencies if you reside in its country.

www.plr.uk.com (U.K.)
www.plr-dpp.ca (Canada)
www.arts.gov.au/books/lending_rights
(Australia)
www.natlib.govt.nz/services/
national-collaborative-services/plr
(New Zealand)

To find out about other countries, visit PLR International at

www.plrinternational.com

Of course, when discussing rights registration, the elephant in the closet is the Book Rights Registry proposed as part of the forthcoming Google Book Settlement. Despite the concerns of some, this registry should prove beneficial to U.S. authors and publishers by providing a convenient way to maintain and protect your rights. For more info, visit

www.googlebooksettlement.com

About Google Books

The Google Books Partner Program offers to publishers a kind of broader-scale version of Amazon's Search Inside. Google Books will index your book for you from a PDF file or a scan, so that the book's contents can be accessed by a Google search. (Lightning Source has done much of the scanning for Google Books.)

Googlers who click on the book's link in results are taken to a Web page on which they can read the relevant page from your book, along with up to 20% of the rest of it, in a percentage you set. The Web page also includes links to Amazon and other places the book can be bought—including your own Web site, if you like. And of course, there are ads, from which Google will gladly share the revenue with you, again if you like.

The online display of your book's pages—with the limit you set—is not restricted to that Google page. Google licenses this feature to retailers like Borders, Books-A-Million, Powell's, Blackwell Bookshop, The Book Depository, and Buy.com, as well as to the international library catalog resource WorldCat. The feature has also been integrated into literary social networking sites like aNobii, weRead, BookJetty, GoodReads, and BookRabbit. And you can even embed it simply and freely in a Web page of your own.

Even so, the benefits to publishers from Google Books have so far been less than spectacular. In fact, I have never heard a self publisher claim a significant advantage from being part of this program. Meanwhile, the program's procedures have been slow, awkward, and hit-and-miss.

In its defense, though, Google has been distracted for years by the lawsuit against its Library Project and by new operations to be made possible by the Google Book Settlement. And some of those operations, like Google Editions, may mean significant new revenue for self publishers.

Eventually, you'll probably want to be part of Google Books. If you'd like to start now, click on the link for publisher info at

books.google.com

3
Working with Lightning

Understand the Model

Lightning Source is something new under the sun, and self publishers sometimes have trouble understanding exactly how Lightning make its profit, and how they make their own. So, let's look at the financial factors for a typical book, namely a black-and-white paperback with color cover.

These figures are from early 2010—but Lightning's charges have been remarkably stable. In fact, the U.S. prices haven't gone up in most of a decade!

Setup and maintenance fees. There are no fees just to set up an account at Lightning. Each book submitted digitally has a very reasonable setup fee for interior and cover combined, plus a fee for a proof copy. In addition, for each book, there's a small annual "catalog fee" for including info in Lightning's database and its electronic feed to booksellers—in other words, for distributing the book. Here are the figures in dollars, pounds, and euros.

Setup	$75	£42	€48
Proof	$30	£21	€25
Catalog	$12	£7	€8

All in all, these fees are minimal, designed not to earn much profit for the company but to encourage you to submit more books.

Printing cost. Printing is charged by the page, with an extra charge per copy for the cover and binding. For paperbacks shorter than 10 inches or 254 mm, printing costs are

Per Copy	$.90	£.70	€.80
Per Page	$.013	£.01	€.011

(Just to make sure the decimal position isn't confusing, that U.S. charge per page is 1.3¢.)

For any taller paperbacks, the charges are

Per Copy	$1.30	£1.00	€1.15
Per Page	$.018	£.015	€.017

Note that there are minimum charges for books with low page counts, and in the U.S., the prices are slightly higher if you're ordering copies for yourself.

These printing charges too are purposely kept low—but with Lightning printing between one and two million copies per month, even a small profit adds up!

List price. This is the book's "cover price"—what the final customer would pay, not counting any discount. You assign this price yourself. Lightning imposes no minimum or maximum limits on it. You're the publisher!

"Wholesale" discount. Lightning is both a printer and a distributor. After printing your book, it buys it from you at a discount off your list price to resell to its "distribution partners"—the select wholesalers and retailers who can order direct from Lightning. This includes Lightning's primary partner, Ingram. Though Lightning Source and Ingram Book Company are sister companies under the same ownership, Ingram has to buy its books from Lightning just like any of the others.

Technically, the discount Lightning takes is a *distributor discount*—a discount you give it for acting as distributor. But Lightning gives this a twist and calls it a "wholesale discount"—because it is the *same* discount that Lightning gives to Ingram and its other distribution partners when it resells the book. In other words, Lightning passes along the *entire* distributor discount you give it and makes money only from the printing.

The most unusual thing about the distributor discount you give to Lightning is, like the list price, you set it yourself. It can be anywhere between 20% and 55%. So, if you don't want to give up any more than 20% as discount to Ingram, Amazon, or Barnes & Noble—you got it!

Another unusual thing about this discount is, even when set at 55%, it's much lower than standard distributor discounts, which typically run around 65%. Lightning is making up for the higher printing costs of print on demand by giving you probably the best distribution deal in the industry.

I'll say much more about discounts later. For now, though, it's important to understand that the discount you set at Lightning is *only* for Lightning and its distribution partners. It is *not* the same discount later given by Ingram, Amazon, or any other wholesale or retail bookseller to its customers.

Because new Lightning publishers so often misunderstand this, they commonly make the mistake of setting their discount at 40%, thinking that any bookstore will be able to buy their books at that discount. In most cases, *that is not the discount the bookstore will get.* Instead, most bookstores will have to order from Ingram at a discount that's 15 to 25 percentage points *lower*—because that's how *Ingram* makes its money.

For instance, if you set your Lightning discount at 40%, the bookstore's discount from Ingram will be only 15%. To make sure the bookstore gets 40%, your Lightning discount would have to be a full 55%.

Your profit. We now have all the ingredients for figuring your profit per copy, apart from the minimal setup fees. And note I said "profit," not "royalties." Authors get royalties, publishers make profit!

Here's the profit formula for any copy that Lightning distributes for you:

List Price - "Wholesale" Discount - Printing Cost =
Your Profit

"Your Profit" is what Lightning sends you, three months after each month's sales report. (The three months wait is for collecting from booksellers.) Note that you never pay shipping on these distributed copies, never pay a handling fee, never get dinged in any other such way. You get the whole amount. Also note that *you send no money to Lightning.* All your expenses for these copies have been deducted before you're paid.

As an example, let's apply this formula to a book of 200 pages, 6 x 9 inches, priced at $15, with the highest possible discount of 55%.

$$\$15 - 55\% - (\$.90 + (200 \times \$.013)) = \$3.25$$

And again with the lowest discount of 20%.

$$\$15 - 20\% - (\$.90 + (200 \times \$.013)) = \$8.50$$

With the highest discount, this is comparable to what you'd make per copy from a distributed book either with a self publishing company or in old-style self publishing. With the lowest discount, it's phenomenally more. And the discount is entirely your choice.

Welcome to the club.

Setting Up Sales

Self publishers using Lightning Source are sometimes confused about how to sell copies of their books to online booksellers like Amazon and BarnesandNoble.com. So, let me make one thing crystal clear: **You do *not* sell your books to online booksellers.**

When you work with Lightning, these booksellers do *not* buy copies from you. They buy them from Lightning or Ingram, but *never* from you directly. All such sales are handled for you, without any involvement on your part.

Let's get even more specific. You do *not* have to sell copies through Amazon Advantage, Amazon's program for small publishers. And considering that Advantage demands a 55% discount, makes you pay shipping, and only pays when the copies are sold, that's about the last thing you'd want to do! In fact, one of the chief benefits of working with Lightning is that it lets you get *around* Advantage.

You also do *not* want to become a Barnes & Noble "vendor of record" just to sell on the Web site. This would require you to accept B&N's standard terms and fulfill direct orders.

You've signed up with Lightning for the best distribution setup available to self publishers today. Let it do its job!

Consider Capabilities

As good a deal as Lightning Source offers, it won't do you any good if your book has requirements that Lightning can't satisfy. So, let's look at some of Lightning's strengths and limitations, starting with what Lightning itself says it can do, as of early 2010. (Check Lightning's current operating manual or a Lightning rep for details and updates.)

For books with black-and-white interiors:

• Covers are paperback (perfectbound) or hardcover. Hardcovers can be stamped cloth or laminated, with or without jackets. Comb binding is not available.

• A wide range of standard U.S. and U.K. trim sizes are offered jointly by Lightning US and Lightning UK, so you can print the same size in both countries. The smallest sizes are 5 × 8 inches and 198 × 129 millimeters (B format), and the largest sizes are 8.25 × 11 inches and 297 × 210 millimeters (A4). *All trim sizes are in portrait mode (vertical orientation).*

• Paperbacks must be between 48 and 828 pages, with spine text permitted only on books of 80 pages or more. Hardcovers must be between 108 and 828 pages. (Minimum page counts are based on pages needed for Lightning's glue binding to hold together.) Note that these are *pages,* not *sheets.* There are two pages to a sheet, front and back.

• Paper choices are cream, 55 lb (75 gsm), and white, 50 lb (85 gsm), both acid-free and archival-quality. (For cream, the maximum page count goes down to 740.) Most covers are 90 lb (240 gsm), laminated.

• Bleeds do not work, because Lightning prints only the portion of your page within trim borders.

• Interior printing is with dry toner, currently on Océ 9200 presses. Cover printing is with oil-based ink on HP Indigo presses.

For books with full-color interiors:

• Covers are paperback only, either perfectbound (glued) or saddle-stitched (stapled). Again, no comb binding.

• Only a few trim sizes are available, with only one square format and none in landscape. The smallest size is 5.5 × 8.5 inches (216 × 140 mm), and the largest size is 8.5 × 11 inches (280 × 216 mm).

• Saddle-stitched books must be between 4 and 48 pages. Perfectbound books must be between 24 and 480 pages. (For fewer than 80 pages, you must omit any text on the spine.)

• Paper is 70 lb (104 gsm) white uncoated, acid-free and archival-quality. Covers are 80 lb (216 gsm), laminated.

• Bleeds are allowed, but must be a minimum of a quarter inch. To ensure reliable gluing of perfectbound books, *no image is allowed within an eighth inch of the gutter*.

• Both interior and cover printing are with oil-based ink on HP Indigo presses.

Lightning can print in any language, as long as you use high-quality fonts and embed them properly in your files. Arranging pages for right-to-left reading, though, doesn't work well, because Lightning automatically adds one to six blank pages to what would otherwise be the end of the book but in this case would be the front. And it doesn't work at all for hardcovers, where binding is done manually and workers can easily get confused.

No special handling is possible, so you cannot package other items with books—discs, printed inserts, or such. You also cannot insert color pages within a black-and-white book. And no specially-defined "spot" colors are allowed.

Though this discussion is basically about Lightning's POD capabilities, Lightning also offers traditional, offset printing for large orders you place directly—1500 copies or more of a paperback, or 750 or more of a hardcover. Lightning uses your same book files for offset as for POD, so there's no extra setup.

OK, that's what Lightning can do. Now, the other question is, how well does it do it?

The quality of print on demand has made huge leaps over the years and will continue to do so. It has evolved from something inferior to what you could get from a desktop laser printer, to a product that most people truly can't distinguish from a traditionally-printed book. And Lightning has kept itself in the vanguard by adopting improvements as they become available. But that doesn't mean no issues remain.

Most discussions of print quality start with the graphics, so we'll start there too. Interior graphics used to be the weakest point of POD, due to the coarseness of the screening—the process that turns continuous-tone images into printable dots. Photos especially looked terrible, and it was best to simply avoid using them. Now, though, Lightning's screening for a black-and-white book has gone up to 106 lines per inch, and there have been other improvements too—like the use of a glossy toner that gives images more depth. Image quality is now good enough that it's no longer a big issue in most cases.*

Still, that screen resolution is a good ways below what's typical for offset book printing—in fact, it's no higher than the top end of what you'd see in a newspaper. Add to that an

---

* If you published books with Lightning before February 2008, the interior halftones probably still don't look that great. That's because, when Lightning upgraded its system of file processing and handling for superior graphics, it didn't automatically update older files. To reap the benefits of the upgrade, submit your interior files for reprocessing via Lightning's normal revision process. (You may instead be able to arrange for Lightning to reprocess your original files, but you'll probably have to pay either way.)

inconsistency in toner levels from book to book—or even from page to page—that causes images to sometimes print lighter and sometimes darker, and you'll understand that black-and-white POD is not a congenial medium for fine art.

What about images in color POD? For book covers as well as books with inside color, Lightning screens at 180 lines per inch, which is certainly high enough for any normal use. For interior color, though, Lightning prints on uncoated paper, which has a limited dynamic range. This makes color photos look dull. It works wonderfully, though, for other types of color graphics, including illustration art and comics.*

Ironically, it works very well also for black-and-white photos. So, if you need high-quality black-and-white, Lightning's color POD can be a good way to go—if you can afford the much higher cost.

What about line drawings, which aren't screened? Lightning's black-and-white books are printed at 600 dots per inch. This is fine enough for most uses, but might not work well for extremely delicate lines. Here, Lightning's color POD is worse, at 300 dots per inch.

Images get all the attention, but in most books, it's the type that's more important. Even while printing at 600 dpi, Lightning's POD type used to be very rough, and delicate typefaces simply didn't work. Today, Lightning's type is a lot smoother, though at the cost of less crispness at its edges. Still, because of inconsistent toner levels, you should avoid delicate typefaces—ones with thin strokes—in very small font sizes.

The glossy toner that Lightning uses to improve graphics also makes type look darker and richer. But it has two unfortunate side effects. One is that new books have a strong chemical odor that some people may find offensive. (It does go away

---

* Lightning has a side business in printing photo books on high-quality paper—but that service isn't available to its book publisher clients!

fairly quickly.) The other is that, under some lighting, the type can produce a glare that makes reading uncomfortable. With offset printing, glare is common from glossy paper—but with Lightning's POD, it comes from the type itself! (Though few people consciously notice the glare, I personally find it troublesome enough that I chose a different company as the primary POD provider for a literary novel of my wife's.)

And the binding? Pages hold firm and spines stay intact, even after many years. Trim dimensions and cover positioning, though, can vary as much as an eighth inch, despite Lightning's quality guarantee of no more than a sixteenth. Covers of thick books may be slightly tilted. And now and then, you'll hear of a cover being attached to the wrong book!*

As you might gather from all the above, the biggest challenge facing Lightning's POD is consistency. Yes, with a perfect sample, few people can tell the difference between POD and traditional printing. The hitch is that not all POD samples are perfect.

To understand why this is true, it's important to realize that a POD operation has little in common with a traditional print shop. In fact, you might better think of it as a glorified copy shop—a Kinko's on steroids.

As at your local copy shop, machine operators can be hired with no previous experience. No one is hovering over the press with a constant critical eye on print densities, or examining type edges under a loupe. A great deal of care and intelligence goes into setting up Lightning's systems and machines, and maintenance is rigorous—but when they're in motion, quality control has to take second place to speed and efficiency.

---

* One Lightning publisher who orders his books in large batches estimates that one out of 300 to 500 Lightning books have mismatched covers. But since copies in large batches may be less prone to error, and since Lightning's average print run is under two copies, this estimate may be low.

The upshot is that Lightning's POD—especially the black-and-white variety—excels with books for which content is more important than appearance. If you keep your expectations in line with that, you will not be disappointed. And if not all your books are perfect, you can consider it the price of wide distribution and flexibility in terms.

By the way, a corollary of Lightning's inconsistency is that it might not be wise to order a huge batch of books at one time. Though Lightning will replace bad copies, you don't want to return most of a large shipment just because one of Lightning's machines had a bad day.

As I said before, Lightning and POD are improving in quality all the time, so consider this a time-limited report card. Not too far down the road, for instance, inkjet presses are expected to replace the current toner-based ones—and that could change everything!

How to Spell *Lightning*

It's spelled "lightning." Not "lightening."
Really. There's no *e*.
Trust me.

Use the Site

Many of your dealings with Lightning Source will be through its Web site, via your home account, which will be based in either the U.S. or the U.K. Here again is the address.

www.lightningsource.com

I'll be giving you tips about the Web site as we go along, but for now, here's a short list of what you can do there.

• Find resources. You'll find operating manuals, technical documents, templates, and more.

• Submit books. The simplest way to submit your book files is right on the Web site—at least if your Internet connection is broadband.

• Change terms and listings. This includes basic info, price, discount, and returnability.

• Get sales reports. If you can't wait till the end of the month, you can view sales figures updated daily.

• Make payments. Use your credit card to pay Lightning's fees and charges.

• Order books. This is for delivery to yourself or to another address of your choice.

That's all in your *home* account. But if you've signed up for direct ordering in both the U.S. and the U.K., you'll have a secondary account with Lightning in the other country—an account just for ordering and paying for books you want printed and shipped from there instead. You'll access this secondary account on *the same Web site*—but just using a second login name assigned to you by Lightning.

Work with Reps

Besides the Web site, you'll also have access to several Lightning representatives assigned to you. You'll find their names and contact info on the first page of the Lightning Web site after you log into your home account—the page called "My Lightning Account at a Glance."

Generally, your Sales Rep will help you set up accounts and distribution, and you might not talk to her often. Your Client Services Rep, on the other hand, is for technical matters and for dealing with individual books, and with her you might be in much more frequent contact. You'll also have a Credit or Finance Rep, in case you have any questions about Lightning's charges.

Client Services Reps are assigned to you on the basis of geography. Their quality varies, of course, and what you get is by the luck of the draw. If you like your rep, bless heaven. If you don't, then take some comfort in the fact that reps are occasionally shuffled, so you'll likely get a different one later. (If you get *really* desperate, a discussion with your Sales Rep might get you reassigned.)

But like her or not, remember one thing: Your Client Services Rep is grossly overworked. One rep told a client she was handling 900 publishers!

Reps continually field inquiries by email and phone, and they don't have much time to spend on any one communication. Subtlety or complexity in your message can easily get lost in the rush. For the best response, keep your inquiries short and simple. If possible, limit your email to a single request or question. If you have more than that, send more than one email!

It should go without saying that you also should treat your rep courteously, even if you feel frustrated. Remember that she's doing her best in a highly demanding job. And don't forget to thank her either, when she has helped you. (By the way, I use "her" and "she" because nearly all Lightning reps are female.)

The best way to use your rep, though, is as little as possible. Most questions can be answered by reading Lightning Source documentation. From the Web site, download the comprehensive Publisher Operating Manual, which has versions for both the U.S. and the U.K. Study it till you've learned everything that applies to you, then keep referring to it, as well as checking the Lightning site for updates. Take advantage too of the various guides and tutorials Lightning makes available—but recognize that these might not be as up-to-date as the Operating Manual.

Also, don't rely on your rep or anyone else at Lightning for basic instruction in publishing and production. Learn your business as well as you can on your own, and if you need help with that, find it elsewhere. An occasional gaffe won't be held against you, but if you really don't have a clue, don't expect Lightning to take up the slack.

Keep in mind that Lightning's main business is with large and medium-sized publishers and with self publishing companies—not with self publishers directly. As more and more self publishers learn of this opportunity, Lightning's direct dealings with them are bound to grow. But if Lightning ever feels that customer support requirements are getting out of hand, it could easily tighten its policy against serving "authors." For the sake of the self publishing community, then, do your homework and don't pester your rep.

P.S. Coming to Lightning in early 2010: Live Chat!

The Ingram Companies

In this book, I use "Ingram" to refer to Ingram Book Company rather than to either of the Ingram-branded entities encompassing both the wholesaler and Lightning Source. But here's the full rundown:

Lightning Source Inc. and Ingram Book Company are operating units of the company Ingram Content Group. For more on Ingram Content Group, visit

www.ingramcontent.com

In turn, Ingram Content Group is part of the umbrella company Ingram Industries. Lightning Source began life as a separate company of Ingram Industries but was brought together with other units in 2008.

4
Dealing with Data

Gather Your Info

Publishing involves handling a good deal of info about your book—basic data and promotional material meant to identify, classify, and describe the book in various ways and for various purposes. Some of this might be placed on the book's front or back cover, and some on the beginning pages of the book—especially on the *copyright page,* or *title verso,* the left-hand page following the title page. It will also be given directly to various services and agencies for their databases and online listings.

Because there's so much info to handle, your best bet is to collect all of it in a single computer file. In fact, you can start this file way at the beginning of your book writing, when you're working out a title. Then add to the file as you go along.

This book info file is not only to keep info handy, but also to let you directly copy from it, so that you can paste its contents into Web forms and your email and your book itself as needed. Copying and pasting is not only more convenient than retyping but also much safer, because you avoid errors—an especial danger with the long strings of numbers you'll have to deal with. *Never retype basic info if you can copy and paste it.*

You have to be careful, though, about the format that the info is in. To accommodate the variety of computer systems that will handle it, your book info file should be in "plain text" or "ASCII," such as is handled in a text editor like Notepad (Windows) or TextEdit (Mac). All quotes should be "straight," and you can't use italics, bolding, special characters, or anything else fancy. In other words, it should be opposite in typography to what you'd put in your book.

Of course, for info you place in your book, you *will* need "curly" quotes, true dashes, italics for emphasis, and so on—so in those cases, you may need to adjust the text after pasting it.

Assign Your ISBN

The most important piece of info belonging to a book is its ISBN—*International Standard Book Number*. As I said before, this is what's used in the book trade to identify each format of each published book, and also the publisher. I've already told you how to acquire a set of these. Now all you need to do is select one of the numbers to use for your book—or one number for each physical format, if you've decided to publish in more than one. (You can assign ISBNs to ebooks too, but that's not required.)

Note that you do *not* have to use the ISBNs from your block in numerical order—you can choose any one of the numbers for any title or format. Also note that, once you use a particular ISBN, you must *not* reuse it on a different book or format, even if the first is out of print.

When dealing with identifiers, it's always informative and helpful to look at how they're put together. Let's take as an example the ISBN for this book:

978-0-938497-46-2

A new ISBN always has exactly thirteen digits. The hyphens can be replaced by spaces, though this is not common in the U.S. The rule when printing the number in the book is to include the hyphens or spaces—but for online forms, you'll most often have to leave them out. So, you should include the number both ways in your book info file for copying.

The ISBN is actually a subset of a worldwide system of product identification called EAN *(European Article Number)*. The "978" prefix you see here identifies this as an ISBN, as opposed to an EAN for any other kind of product. Now that

"978" numbers for ISBNs are running out, you'll start also seeing "979" to mean the same.

The "0" is a country code, indicating the country or country "group" in which the publisher is located. Groups are largely created on the basis of common language—both "0" and "1" being code for "most English-speaking countries." Also, countries with regions where different languages are spoken might belong to more than one group, as does Canada, with its English- and French-speaking areas. Still, the country code is based primarily on geography, not language. If you live in the U.S., your code will be "0" or "1," regardless of the language you write in.

When you connect the next clump of digits to the ones before, you get my *publisher prefix,* "978-0-938497." All my books carry ISBNs with this prefix. In fact, if I want to see all my self-published books on Amazon or Ingram's ipage or BowkerLink, all I have to do is search on either "9780938497" or "9780938497*" (with the asterisk at the end acting as a "wild card").

The next two digits of my ISBN, "46," identify a single title in a particular edition and format—in this case, *POD for Profit* in its one and only edition and its one and only format. The fact that there are two digits here shows I have a set of 100 ISBNs, because that's how many books you can identify with two digits—100 books, counted from "00" to "99."

A larger publisher would normally have a shorter prefix, leaving more digits to identify titles, as in this ISBN of one of my picture books from Atheneum, an imprint of Simon & Schuster.

978-0-689-84259-7

Here, the prefix is 978-0-689, and the book identifier is 84259—a five-digit identifier indicating a set of 100,000

ISBNs! And on the other end of the scale, a publisher smaller than I am might have an ISBN like this:

978-0-9723801-1-9

Here, the prefix leaves only one digit to identify books—ten of them, from "0" to "9."

The final digit of my ISBN, "1," is a *check digit.* It's calculated using a formula involving all the other digits. This lets computer programs check that there are no errors in the number they're given. To stick to a single check digit, a calculated result of "10" is represented as "X." Be careful, now—this is a *capital* "X."

The check digit can reveal most errors but not all—for that, you would need *two* digits. So, this puts a little extra responsibility on you to get the ISBN right. About the last thing you want is to publish a book with an inaccurate ISBN! Again, never retype when you can copy and paste.

The ISBN is sometimes printed specially on the back cover—but since it will appear there anyway in the bar code, there's really no need. It also appears on the book's copyright page. Here's how it looks in this book:

ISBN 978-0-938497-46-2

If you're publishing your book in more than one format—which, for reasons discussed in *Aiming at Amazon,* I do *not* advise—the best idea is to list the ISBNs for *every* format on *all* the copyright pages, telling what each ISBN is for—paperback, hardcover, whatever. This way, you don't need a different copyright page for each format and can keep the entire book content identical for all. For instance, here's what appears in a children's book I published in both hardcover and paperback (against my own advice).

ISBN 978-0-938497-34-9 (Library binding)
ISBN 978-0-938497-36-3 (Paperback)

In the past, all ISBNs had ten digits. The "978" prefix for the EAN was added to the bar code on the cover (with a change in the check digit)—but since it applied to *all* books, it was not included in the ISBN itself. But now that the additional prefix of "979" is needed to avoid running out of EANs for books, all thirteen digits must be included in the ISBN itself.

You'll still see 10-digit ISBNs around for a while—and during the years of transition, they were supposed to be printed *along with* 13-digit numbers—but they're now obsolete. So, now you should list *only* the 13-digit ISBN in or on any new book. And *don't* label it "ISBN-13"! That's redundant and bad form.

If you have any 10-digit ISBNs from before, you can use them after simply converting them to 13-digit. There are many forms on the Web that will do that for you automatically, adding the "978" and recalculating the check digit. Here's a handy one from the U.S. Library of Congress for converting individual ISBNs.

pcn.loc.gov/isbncnvt.html

For bulk conversions, you can use this one from the International ISBN Agency.

www.isbn-international.org/ia/isbncvt

Though there's no longer any place for a 10-digit ISBN inside a new book, you'll find they still linger in various parts of the book trade. Sometimes this might be under the name SKU (*Stock Keeping Unit*). Other times, you'll find that the 10-digit form is called ISBN, while the 13-digit form is called EAN.

Amazon still uses the 10-digit ISBN as an ASIN *(Amazon Standard Identification Number),* its chief product identifier.

So, for anywhere the 10-digit form might be needed, keep that too in your book info file—both with and without hyphens or spaces. The Library of Congress form at the address above can figure out 10-digit ISBNs from 13-digit ones as well as the other way around.

Also, be aware that not everyone in publishing has yet figured out that the "978" or "979" must now be part of publisher prefixes. If you ever fill out an online form that asks for your prefix but doesn't accept the whole thing, just leave off those first three digits.

Technically, if you change the content of your book in a significant way, you're supposed to issue a new edition with a new ISBN for each format. But as I discussed in *Aiming at Amazon,* the ease of revision that comes with print on demand is weakening this standard. To save money and effort—as well as to preserve a book's position on Amazon—some self publishers revise a book without changing any ISBN.

What if you're moving a book to Lightning from another POD provider? In general, it's best to treat the book as a new edition with a new ISBN. But for details, see the special section "Moving to Lightning" later in this book.

Set the Year

Your book's *copyright year* will be associated with it in almost any listing, to let people know when it appeared and how old it is. It's the book's official year of publication.

Most often, it's also the *actual* year of publication—but if you're close to the end of a year, it's standard to list the upcoming year instead. That way, your book doesn't quickly look older than it really is. In any case, the copyright year should match the year of your official *publication date,* which I'll discuss later.

Generally, the copyright year appears in the book only on the *copyright page*—the page named after it—which is normally the *title verso,* the page following the title page. It appears there in the context of a *copyright statement,* such as the one in this book:

Copyright © 2010 by Aaron Shepard

It doesn't have to be exactly that way, but that's the general idea.

If the book has any content previously published, or if the book itself has been revised since its original publication, you could include more than one year, like so:

Copyright © 2006, 2008–2010 by Aaron Shepard

If more than one year is included in the statement, which one is the copyright year? Always the latest—the year that appears last in the statement.

In the U.S., the copyright statement used to be required to establish your copyright in the book. That's no longer true—but the statement is still a convenient and conventional way to announce your copyright year, and yourself as the ultimate rights holder. It also warns away people who think a book that lacks the notice is not protected!

Guide Booksellers

It's not always easy for booksellers to know where a book should be shelved or listed, so they've developed classifications to help them. The U.S. and the U.K. each has its own system, and you might need to deal with both.

In the U.S., the dominant system is the BISAC Subject Headings List. BISAC stands for Book Industry Systems Advisory Committee, which is part of the Book Industry Study Group (BISG), a trade association. Often you'll see the acronym BASIC in place of BISAC—who knows why?—but it's referring to the same thing.

To find your book's BISAC code, just go to the BISG site at

www.bisg.org

and click through to the online headings list.

In the U.K., the BIC Standard Subject Categories system is used instead. BIC is Book Industry Communication, another trade association, on the Web at

www.bic.org.uk

There you can download a complete list of headings or use the online selection tool.*

In either system, find as many categories as can possibly apply to your book, then list them in order of importance. You'll need these categories in your book info file to submit for online listings. The number you can enter is usually limited, so just start at the top of your list and work down. It's also

---

* Version 2 of the BIC category scheme was released in April 2006. If you classified any books by the earlier scheme, you might consider reclassifying them. Or not.

standard to print the book's primary category in a corner of your back cover—but for a book aimed at online sales, you can skip that.

Assist Librarians

Like booksellers, librarians can often use some help in knowing how to handle your book. In the U.S., one source of such help is an identifier called the *Library of Congress Control Number*, or LCCN. (You might sometimes see its older name, *Library of Congress Catalog Number*.)

While ISBNs identify each format of each edition, an LCCN identifies just the edition itself, in any and all of its formats. The number is also used to access any cataloging data generated for your book by the Library of Congress or any of various library services. Though you might not plan to market your book to libraries, it's likely that at least some will pick it up—so it's always good practice to obtain an LCCN.

LCCNs are issued only by the Library of Congress. There are several ways to get one, but the best for self publishers is to ask for what's called a *Preassigned Control Number* (PCN)—simply, an LCCN that's issued before your book comes out. There's no charge for this service, and it's available to all U.S. publishers of any size. To sign up for the program and apply for a number, visit the Preassigned Control Number Program at

pcn.loc.gov

When you apply for the number, submit your book info as you expect it to appear in the book. If there's anything you're not yet sure of, just give your best guess. All info will be checked against the book when you later send the required review copy.

Here's the number for *POD for Profit*.

2009911873

The "2009" is the year the number was assigned, *not* the copyright year—which in this case was 2010. The rest identifies my application individually within that year. In the past, a hyphen was inserted after the year, but new numbers no longer include that.

You'll normally get your LCCN within a day—not a week, as warned on the site.

As with the ISBN, a new LCCN is supposed to replace the old whenever a book is changed significantly. But also as with the ISBN, this standard is slipping under the pressure of print on demand.

On the copyright page of many U.S. books, in place of a simple LCCN, you'll see full library cataloging data in the style of the Library of Congress. This *Cataloging in Publication* (CIP) may be supplied to established U.S. publishers by the Library of Congress itself, or to smaller, newer publishers by an independent service.

Unfortunately, the Library of Congress program is limited to publishers with three or more authors, and "books published on demand" are specifically ruled out. (Yes, they can easily tell when they later examine the book copy you send, because of Lightning's markings on the last page.) But if you'd like to check for changes in requirements or find other info, go to the Cataloging in Publication Program at

cip.loc.gov

Self publishers are sometimes told that CIP is essential for selling a book to U.S. libraries. This is no longer true. Librarians today can most often obtain cataloging data for a book over the Internet, especially if they have the LCCN. In fact, librarians themselves now discuss whether printing CIP in books is even worthwhile! So, unless you're working with a distributor that requires it, there's little reason for you to pay anyone for cataloging.

You also hear that U.S. libraries may buy books based only on CIP data received by subscription, in order to fill specific needs. Though there may be some truth to this, it's unlikely they'd buy books that way from publishers they don't know—and I have yet to identify any small publisher who claims to have had the benefit of this. In any case, this refers to CIP data from the Library of Congress only—and if you go POD, you can't get that.

Setting aside CIP, though, what you might consider providing in your book is the appropriate subject headings from the Library of Congress classification system. Your suggested headings can help librarians guide readers to your book. (For more info, see "LC Subject Headings" following this section.)

Outside the U.S., the situation regarding library info can be very different, first off because most national libraries provide CIP data even to self publishers. Here are links for eligibility and other CIP info in several countries.

> **www.bl.uk/bibliographic/cip.html** (U.K.)
> **www.collectionscanada.gc.ca/cip** (Canada)
> **www.nla.gov.au/services/CIP.html** (Australia)
> **www.natlib.govt.nz/services/get-advice/**
> **publishing/cataloguing-in-publication**
> (New Zealand)

For others, search the Web for "CIP" and the country name.

LC Subject Headings

Though it's no longer necessary or convenient in the U.S. to outfit your book with Cataloging in Publication (CIP), you might still want to include the appropriate Library of Congress subject headings. These are the phrases by which people may find your book in library catalogs based on the LC system—generally, the catalogs of university, government, and professional libraries, not only in the U.S. but in English-speaking countries around the world. (Public libraries normally use the Dewey Decimal System instead.)

If the cataloging librarian for one of these libraries doesn't assign the best headings to your book, it might not be found by library patrons. Suggestions you place on your book's copyright page are at least likely to be seen and considered when the book is cataloged.*

As an example, here are the headings I assembled for my book *Perfect Pages:*

> Desktop publishing
> Self-publishing—Handbooks, manuals, etc.
> Publishers and publishing—Handbooks, manuals, etc.
> Microsoft Word
> Book design
> Type and type-founding
> Word processing

---

* Amazon too used to assign Library of Congress subject headings to books and would sometimes accept publisher suggestions for them. The headings were shown on the book's detail page and were also used as keywords for Amazon search. Though you still see older assignments displayed, Amazon no longer assigns LC headings to new books.

Don't think that LC subject headings are only for nonfiction! Fiction too gets classified. In fact, the list for my wife, Anne's, second novel, *Pacific Avenue,* is even longer than the one above.

> Race relations—Fiction
> Interracial marriage—Fiction
> Sudden infant death syndrome—Fiction
> Vietnam War, 1961–1975—Veterans—Fiction
> Veterans—Family relationships—Fiction
> Post-traumatic stress disorder—Fiction
> New Orleans (La.)—Fiction
> Baton Rouge (La.)—Fiction
> San Pedro (Los Angeles, Calif.)—Fiction
> Puppets—Fiction

Figuring out the best LC subject headings can be tricky, especially since the classification system is frequently revised and the headings themselves can change. What's more, cataloging can be idiosyncratic, so that even experienced librarians may classify the same book in different ways.

Your best bet is to access the online catalog of a major library or system that uses LC cataloging. My own favorite source of subject headings is MELVYL, the search service of the University of California. This service lets you search through all U.C. libraries or through major libraries worldwide. Find it at

melvyl.worldcat.org

For the online catalog of the Library of Congress itself, go to

catalog.loc.gov

Look up as many books as possible on the same or similar subjects as yours, keeping a special eye on newer books. Try to find the headings used most often for your subject, then copy them *exactly*. Unless there's an obvious error, don't change a single punctuation mark or form of spelling, even if it's badly outdated or politically incorrect.

Though LC subject headings are used in English-speaking countries worldwide, the headings are often supplemented nationally for subjects of more local interest. So, if you're outside the U.S. and looking for headings for such subjects, be sure to check library catalogs from your own country.

Reveal Your Content

A compelling description of your book can have many uses. In the book itself, it can appear on the back cover or on the book's first page, before the title page. But you'll also be including it often when submitting book info online.

Don't just summarize contents. Think of a pithy way to intrigue or appeal to a reader. For nonfiction, sometimes you'll find an effective passage in the book's introduction—in fact, I often purposely write a passage there that I can later adapt. For fiction, tell just enough to leave the reader hanging, so they'll want to find out what happens.

Descriptions should come in at least two lengths, for use as the situation requires. One version should be only a paragraph, the other should be two or three.

You'll also need a paragraph about yourself as author. Make it impressive, but not pompous, and don't list a lot of honors that aren't relevant to the book. (For the book itself, this can go on the back cover and/or a back page.)

The more you can show to a customer online, the more likely you are to make a sale. Some online forms allow you to submit a table of contents and/or an excerpt, so it's good to keep these also in your book info file. Remember to convert them to plain text if you're drawing them directly from your book.

For nonfiction, the table of contents can sway the customer with detail and thoroughness. For fiction, it can intrigue. For a collection, it can precisely describe your content. Because this one is only for online display, you don't have to construct it just like the one in your book. Leave out page numbers, and format as simply and compactly as possible. Since you can't vary type size or style, distinguish higher-level headings with capital letters.

For your excerpt, choose a brief passage that both represents your book at its best and leaves the reader wanting more. You might also prepare a second, longer excerpt, in case that's accepted.

At times, you might be asked to supply keywords that should bring up your book in a search. It's always best to work out a list ahead of time and keep it in your book info file, to avoid missing something in the rush.

Create Your Images

When you submit your book to Lightning Source, it will produce a cover image that will be sent to Ingram and Nielsen BookData, and from there to Amazon and other booksellers. You will even be able to download this image (as I'll explain later) to send anywhere else it's needed.

This image, though, might not be optimal. For one thing, Lightning may have been careless about getting the color right. You might also prefer not to use your actual cover for the image but instead a simpler, bolder version of it. (I discuss this in detail in *Aiming at Amazon*.)

For such reasons, you might want to produce your own cover image, both to send where Lightning's does not go and to replace Lightning's where it does. Though each place you'll send it will list its own technical requirements for images, the following specs will probably satisfy them all.

> Face-on view (not angled or "3D")
> No border (unless background is white)
> JPEG format (high-quality, low compression)
> 72 ppi (or dpi) resolution
> 9 inches max. height or width (648 pixels @ 72 ppi)
> RGB color mode
> sRGB color space
> 24-bit color depth (8 bits per channel)

The cover image file should be named with the ISBN (without hyphens or spaces), along with the file type extension. For instance, my JPEG cover image file for *POD for Profit* is named

> 9780938497462.jpg

As explained in *Aiming at Amazon,* the optimal shape for a cover image on Amazon is a square. Elsewhere, though, the optimal shape is most often a vertical rectangle. In some cases, it's the Web page layout that favors this shape, while in others, the service may simply be more vigilant than Amazon in representing the book accurately.

So, whether or not you develop a separate, square image for Amazon, you'll probably want one image closer to the book's actual shape. You can standardize your rectangle, though, for convenience. For example, for each book I publish, I create two cover images—one for Amazon at 9 × 9 inches, and another for general use at 6 × 9.

Knowing where to submit cover images can get complicated, because of the way they're forwarded from one service or bookseller to another. I'll discuss the various entry points as we go along.

5
Going to Market

Choose a Pub Date

Now let's talk about basic marketing decisions you'll need to make before sending your book to Lightning Source.

One thing you'll have to think about is your book's *publication date*. In traditional publishing, this is oddly enough *not* the date the book goes on sale, but rather an official birthday that can be adjusted for marketing purposes. It's something like the Grand Opening of a store that may already have been open for weeks.

The main function of this promotional "pub date" is to act as an anchor for reviews. Newspaper and magazine reviews and other media attention, if any, are supposed to appear on or near the pub date. Major book trade and library journal reviews are supposed to appear *before* the pub date, so that bookstores and libraries can have big books ready before everyone else finds out about them and comes looking.

Since you're self publishing, your book is not likely to get much of this kind of attention—and when you're aiming at Amazon, it won't really need it. What's more, specifying a future pub date when submitting your book to Lightning can cause listing glitches at some booksellers, even while Lightning and some booksellers ignore the pub date and start selling the book as soon as it's ready. (It's possible to set up your book at Lightning for printing only and add distribution later, but this can cause glitches at Lightning itself.)

For these reasons, I recommend you *forget* about setting a "promo" pub date and instead adopt a "working" pub date—a date on or near when you submit the book to Lightning. It's fine to adjust that date slightly forward or back to neaten it up—say, to the first day of a month. But to make sure it falls ahead of when you accept Lightning's proof, don't set it to more than a few days after Lightning will have your files.

But what if you really, really, *really* want to use a pub date as a target for media attention? Again, I do not recommend giving a future date to Lightning—but you can always set *dual* pub dates.

Under this scheme, a working pub date would go to Lightning when you set up your book—and from there go to Ingram, Amazon, and other booksellers—while a future, promo pub date would go to reviewers and other media contacts. Listing services like Bowker and Nielsen too should get the working pub date, to make sure no bookseller waits longer than needed to list the book as available. But with these services, if you like, you can later change the working pub date to the promo one, after both dates have passed.

Be careful with this scheme, though. You don't want more than about a month's difference between the two dates, because major reviewers might consider you dishonest if they discover it. And of course, make sure the promo pub date matches the copyright year printed in your book!

You should also avoid setting your promo pub date prematurely. It's all too common a mistake of new self publishers to commit themselves to a date by which the book *must* be available through major channels, and then to time their publishing efforts closely to meet that date.

Unfortunately, the world of POD does not run that smoothly or efficiently, and you must also take into account your own learning curve. Nowadays, I figure on about a month between when I send my book to Lightning and when it's fully ready to promote. A newcomer can expect two to three times that. To be safe, then, it's best to wait to set any promo pub date till the book is on sale and satisfactorily listed online.

Publishers who use promo pub dates must take care to schedule publication at optimum times of year. They must also delay publication for months to wait for major reviews. If you take my advice and stick with a working pub date only, you can publish whenever your book is ready. It's never too early to make your book available, and your promotion can follow whenever the time is right.

Lightning also lets you set a *street date*—but apparently only because there's a slot for it in the Ingram database. Street dates are used by big publishers pushing big books, and are meant as the day on which bookstores and online booksellers are allowed to start selling—generally, on or near the pub date. Without a street date, a book goes on sale as soon as it's placed in stock.

For a self publisher, no one pays attention to a street date, and it would be pointless if they did. So just ignore that.

Set a Discount

When I say "discount," you might automatically think of the discounts that retailers like Amazon offer their customers. But that's only one form of discount. The retailer too gets a discount, and so does any other business that stands between the publisher and the customer in the supply chain.

In each case, the discount is stated as a percentage of the *list price*. That's the publisher's "suggested retail price" (SRP), which is usually shown on a book's back cover—in other words, the book's price with no discount at all. For instance, if a book with a $10 *list* price was sold at a discount of 40%, the *discounted* price would be $6.00.

List price	$10.00
Discount (40% of list)	−$4.00
Discounted price	$6.00

In the book industry, there are two general types of discount. *Standard discounts* are based on the fact that bookstores have to make a profit of about 40% of the list price on most books sold if they're going to pay their general business expenses and do all right. So, a standard discount that a publisher gives to a retailer ordering books is around 40%.

But then there are the others in the chain, starting with the wholesalers. These businesses stock books from many publishers to resell to bookstores with convenient one-stop ordering. Typically, a bookstore would go to a wholesaler for books to refill stock or for any other books needed in small quantities or in a hurry. To give the retailer its normal 40% discount, a wholesaler must buy its books at a higher one. So, a standard discount that a publisher gives to a wholesaler is normally 55%.

There's one more tier: the distributors. These outfits normally represent a collection of publishers too small to handle their own nationwide sales. Distributors have salespeople and take orders from both bookstores and wholesalers. To give the others their normal discounts, distributors must get a discount from the publisher of 65% to 70%—about two-thirds off the price of the book. That doesn't leave a whole lot for the publisher! But you don't have to worry about conventional distributors while working with Lightning Source, because Lightning takes their place *without* taking their cut.

The other kind of discount is the *short discount*. Traditionally, this has been used by publishers aiming at the education and library markets—publishers whose books may be more expensive to produce and who don't have to sell through so many tiers, if any. The publisher offers the same short discount to any retailer *or* wholesaler that buys the book, and it's usually around 20% to 25%. Obviously, the publisher gets to keep quite a bit more of the money this way.

Any publisher can offer either kind of discount. But unless you offer a standard discount (or greater), your book will generally not be stocked by bookstores, because they can't make enough (or any) money from it. And it generally won't be stocked by wholesalers, because they know that the bookstores won't carry it. And if it's not stocked by the wholesalers, then bookstores will probably figure that ordering a copy is too much hassle, even if a customer comes in and asks for one—assuming the bookstore can figure out how to order it at all.

What's worse for you, if your book isn't at the wholesalers, Amazon won't carry it or usually even list it unless you sign on with Amazon Advantage or CreateSpace—and that would kind of defeat the whole purpose, wouldn't it, since you'd be giving

Amazon a discount between 40% and 55% anyway. So, you're more or less stuck with standard discounts.

Or you are unless you're distributed by Lightning Source.

One of Lightning's gifts to self publishers is that you do *not* have to give a discount of 55% or more to get into Ingram. *All* Lightning books are automatically carried by Ingram *and* shown as perpetually in stock, *no matter which kind of discount they have.*

With Lightning, the choice is up to you. You can set your "wholesale" discount—the one Lightning gives to Ingram and other booksellers ordering directly—anywhere down to 20%. In fact, your discount can be different for each book, or even for each country for each book. Plus, you can change it whenever you want!*

But exactly what happens if you set a short discount? Let's see how this plays out at Ingram.

Ingram doesn't publicize its guidelines for discounts, but its practices seem pretty consistent. If your discount at Lightning is 55%, Ingram gives retailers a base discount of 40%. For a 50% Lightning discount, Ingram gives 35%. In other words, Ingram takes 15% of your list price as its own cut.

But once you enter the realm of short discounts, Ingram's discounts to retailers drop sharply. At this point, Ingram increases its own cut to 25%—an anachronistic practice from the days before POD, when a short discount meant higher capital investment and greater risk for Ingram. A Lightning discount of 40%—often set by new self publishers who believe bookstores will get the full discount—yields an Ingram discount

---

* There's an exception to all that. If you already have an Ingram account and supply books directly at an agreed discount, you have to stick to it for your Lightning books too. So, if you want to control the discount you're giving, don't deal with Ingram except through Lightning Source!

of only 15%. And for a Lightning discount of 20% to 25%, Ingram's base discount is exactly zero.*

You may be wondering, when Ingram offers no discount, how can a bookstore make any money from selling that book?

Generally speaking, it can't. And in most cases, it should not expect to. Bookstores are used to "special ordering" single copies to fill customer requests, for which they normally get no discount from a publisher—and with self-published books, special ordering is almost all they ever do. It's only when they buy a book in quantity or when they stock it that they expect a substantial discount.

Amazon, of course, *does* sell many Lightning books in quantity. But Amazon is also a special case when it comes to ordering. Unlike most U.S. booksellers, Amazon.com is not limited to ordering Lightning books from Ingram. Amazon also has a direct line into Lightning. Once Amazon receives enough orders for your book to show customer demand—and it doesn't take more than two or three—it will probably decide to go to Lightning and order the book to stock its own warehouses. And Lightning will give Amazon the full discount you've specified. In fact, it's possible that Amazon receives additional discounting as well—say, a discount for quick payment, coming out of Lightning's own pocket.

But Amazon's case is even more special than that, because of its arrangement with Ingram for *drop shipping*. Here's how it works: If an Amazon customer orders your book and Amazon has no copies in stock—because it either isn't stocking the book or has temporarily run out—it still wants to get the book to the customer as promptly as possible. So, it gets Ingram to *drop*

---

* Lightning documentation defines *short discount* as 47% and below—so presumably that's the exact figure Ingram uses as its dividing line. By contrast, Baker & Taylor treats even 50% as a short discount, at that point offering retailers a discount of only 20%.

ship it—in other words, to send it directly to the customer with Amazon's packaging and paperwork. And this arrangement most likely comes with special pricing from Ingram.

So, it's more than possible Amazon does make money—or at least *can* make money—from short discount books, whether ordered from Lightning or from Ingram. In fact, Amazon might be making as much from short discount books as from others that it gets at a higher discount and then discounts deeply!

But all that is what a short discount means to *Amazon*. Here in a nutshell is what it means to *you*: For any publisher working with Lightning Source and aiming at Amazon, a short discount is the very best way to maximize profit. For most books, it's the only really logical policy.

Most of my own publishing success has been built on the short discount, and many—if not most—Lightning publishers now use it. That includes most of the big self publishing companies like AuthorHouse and Lulu.com. Without setting some kind of short discount on their books, these companies would not make enough money to stay in business.

The fact is, with anything but a short discount, you're simply giving away money. To illustrate this, let me tell you a story about my first big book on Amazon, *The Business of Writing for Children*.

I originally priced this book at $12 and told Lightning to set my wholesale discount at 50%. My idea with this was to give Amazon a fair profit when it ordered from Ingram—which was at that time the only way Amazon could get Lightning books. I also wanted to encourage bookstores to stock the book, which I figured they'd do after customers saw it on Amazon and went to the store to ask for it—a common practice especially in Amazon's early years.

At the same time, with the discount Amazon then offered on most books, its customers were paying around $10 for mine, which I figured was optimum. And with a production cost at Lightning of $2.30 per copy, I was making a net profit of $3.70.

List price	$12.00
Discount (50% of list)	−$6.00
Gross profit	$6.00
Printing cost	−$2.30
Net profit	$3.70

It was a reasonable enough strategy, and the book was selling and earning well enough. But after a while I realized two things: First, bookstores were indeed ordering the book in response to customer request—but as far as I could tell, they were *not* stocking it. In fact, after years of my book being an Amazon bestseller, I have yet to learn of *any* bookstore stocking that book. So I was giving the stores a standard discount for nothing.

Second, Amazon was *not* making a "fair profit" from my book. In fact, if you counted Amazon's operating costs, it was making *no* profit from it. What it was doing was taking my discount, then turning around and giving as much of it as it could to its customers. Amazon was intentionally operating at a loss and providing huge discounts to customers so it could undercut traditional bookstores.

So, I took a look at that money Amazon was passing along to its customers, and at that money being kept by bookstores who weren't stocking my book, and I says to myself, says I, "You know, I'd rather keep that money in my own pocket."

So I did. I told Lightning to change my wholesale discount to 25%. That would have nearly doubled my profits—but I also wanted my pricing to remain optimal, and Amazon was then offering no discount on short-discount books. So, I also lowered the book's list price to an even $10. With these figures, my clear profit was $5.20 per copy—an increase of over 50%.

List price	$10.00
Discount (25% of list)	−$2.50
Gross profit	$7.50
Printing cost	−$2.30
Net profit	$5.20

How did this affect my book on Amazon? The discount was removed, so customers now paid a full list price of $10 instead of a discounted price of roughly the same.

That's all.

There was no penalty, no scream of outrage, no subtle undercutting or loss of position in search results, and no noticeable loss of sales. My book was the #1 children's writing guide on Amazon before the change, and that's exactly where it stayed afterwards. Meanwhile, I was making hundreds more dollars per month.*

At that time, Ingram not only offered no discount to retailers on short discount books, it also added a 5% *surcharge* to ones at 20%. This surcharge was passed on by Amazon to its customers, tacked onto the list price. That's why I went no lower than 25%. Much later, though, I discovered that Ingram had stopped applying the surcharge. So, I increased my profit even more by moving most of my books to 20%—again with no ill effect.

Amazon's own approach to giving discounts has varied widely over the years. At this writing, even short-discount

---

* In the last half of 2007, it did look like Amazon was for the first time discriminating against short-discount books. But this was at last fixed through the good graces of an Amazon engineer, who reported it was due to software error. There has been no hint of discrimination since then.

Lightning books, if they're over $10 and maintain at least moderate sales, are being discounted 10%—and sometimes even more, apparently in response to lower, competing prices for new copies in Marketplace. Obviously, the fear of many self publishers that Amazon will "resent" the short discount on a book or even refuse to sell it is completely unfounded.

In fact, judging from some of its pricing practices, Amazon appears to no longer care whether it makes or loses money on any particular book. In other words, Amazon sees its *collective* profit margin on books as more important than margins on individual ones. If Amazon makes more money on some books, it doesn't mind losing it on others.

That is, if it cares about making money on book sales at all. Amazon execs have stated that Amazon is concerned with margins not for any particular kind of product but for the company as a whole.* In other words, though Amazon no longer operates at a loss overall, it may *still* be willingly breaking even or even losing money on book sales, now as a loss leader for the rest of its business.

That business now includes sales of many higher-priced items in the areas of electronics and computers. It includes exorbitantly-priced book promotions set up for major publishers—promotions that Amazon can now strong-arm publishers into purchasing on the strength of Amazon's sales volume. And it includes fees charged to Marketplace vendors, who sell on Amazon to take advantage of its high traffic.

So, there's no point fretting over whether Amazon can make money off your book. Amazon can take care of its own profit, while you take care of yours. And a short discount continues to be the keystone for maximizing that profit.

---

* In "Kindle Drives Amazon to Big Third Quarter," *Publishers Weekly,* Oct. 22, 2009.

Let's be clear, though, about one thing: You can't set a short discount unless you're thoroughly prepared to Forget Bookstores—the first principle, as always, of my publishing plan. Those bookstores will still order your book to fill customer requests. But for the books that a store stocks, it needs a discount of around 40%—and to provide that, your Lightning book would need a standard discount.*

Short-discount books are not universally welcomed among online sellers either. In 2009, Borders.com became the first—and so far, the only—major online bookseller to stop offering short-discount Lightning books.†

The hard truth is, there is no single set of terms and policies that's optimal for every possible bookselling situation. You need to choose your main focus and let other situations work themselves out as they may. My own choice, and the one I recommend as most profitable for most self publishers, is to aim at Amazon with a short discount of 20% at Lightning Source.

But whatever you do, don't "compromise" by setting a discount at Lightning midway *between* 20% and 55%—a common error of new self publishers. You lose much of the benefit of the short discount without gaining any of the benefits of a standard one. Once again, that's just giving away money!

---

* Ironically, now that Amazon offers most Lightning short-discount books at a discount of 10%—in some cases with free shipping—many bookstores are special ordering those books from Amazon instead of Ingram. They make a profit after all! (Thanks for that tip-off to Bruce Batchelor of Agio Publishing House.)

† Actually, Borders.com didn't stop offering such Lightning books that were stocked by Baker & Taylor—but around the same time, B&T stopped stocking any Lightning books at all and resorted to ordering them only to fill backorders.

Set a Price

In general, the key to pricing your book for Amazon sales is to make sure the customer will pay no more for your book than for most of its competitors, and preferably less. In other words, your book's price should be as low or lower *after any discounts of Amazon's.* So, you need to consider both your book's *list* price—the official price you set at Lightning Source—and Amazon's *selling* price.

As an example, let's take the pricing of my book *Aiming at Amazon.** Typically, major books about self publishing list at around $20, and because they're on standard discounts, Amazon sells them for around $13.50. I want my book to sell a bit lower than that, but I know its short discount will currently earn it only about 10% discount on Amazon. So, I list my book at Lightning at $14, giving it an Amazon selling price of $12.60.

Of course, for this approach to work, you need to be up-to-date on how Amazon discounts short-discount books. To check that, you might look on Amazon at current discounts for books from my own Shepard Publications, or ask in the pod_publishers group on Yahoo. But whatever Amazon seems to be doing, be prepared to adjust your list price if things don't work as expected, or if they change. (Don't be too hasty, though. Discounts or the lack of them can sometimes change within days.)

Though meeting the competition is the main factor in setting a price, it's not the only one. For instance, you should aim to make the customer feel they've gotten good value for their money from your particular book. Page count and production

---

* The pricing examples in this section are from late 2009 or earlier and may not reflect current pricing for my books.

quality may be factors in this. Above all, you don't want any customer reviewer saying your book isn't worth what they paid.

Amazon's Super Saver Shipping is also a consideration. With this feature, Amazon.com offers free shipping on orders totaling $25 or more. (Amazon actually says "over $25," but exactly $25 will do.) If you want to encourage customers to buy your book along with others of similar interest, it's sometimes worth raising your target price a bit to help the customer reach the $25 tipping point. For instance, if your book would go well with books at $12.79 and $12.98, it may sell better at $12.25 than at $12.00. Likewise, if you have two complementary books of your own, you might try to make their combined prices reach $25. Again, those figures are *after* any expected discount.

People do enjoy discounts, which can impel them to buy at once instead of waiting for another opportunity, when the discount might not be available. Presently, Amazon seems to mostly be saving its discounts for books with list prices over $10.00. So, for instance, your book might sell better if listed at $11.00 with a 10% discount from Amazon than it would at $10.00 with none, even though the selling price would be roughly the same. Not to mention that your profit per copy would increase! (Memo to self: Try this with *The Business of Writing for Children*.)

Beyond all that, try to develop a general feel for what people want to pay. I greatly increased the sales of my book *How to Love Your Flute* when I dropped my price from $12 to $10 (in the days before Amazon discounted my books). The difference of two dollars wasn't that much, but $10 is a psychological dividing line for many potential purchases. So, at the lower price, I wound up making more from the book's total sales. Another dividing line seems to lie around $12.50, and I've aimed for that selling price for some of my books—

especially when doing so fits into the "free shipping" strategy mentioned above.

Of course, you also want to charge enough to feel that publishing the book was worth your investment. Don't overcharge the customer, but also don't underpay yourself!

Finally, you might want to vary the price over the life of the book. For instance, you could start with a low price to help build market share before raising it to your ultimate target. And as a timely or trendy book wanes in appeal, you could lower the price from its high point to keep it attractive.

If you've read or practiced other approaches to figuring prices, you may be surprised that I'm more interested in enhancing competitiveness and customer appeal than in regulating profit margins. That's because there's a lot more latitude when pricing for print on demand—as long as your book isn't too long and you stick to a short discount. Even though production costs are higher with POD, you're keeping more money for yourself, overhead is lower, and you have no costs of shipping and handling. So, you don't need to pinch pennies.

Traditionally, publishers are told they must price their books at eight times the cost of production to make a profit. For short-discount POD through Lightning Source, just three or four times does nicely. In fact, you can make a profit at two times or less.

So far, I've focused on U.S. pricing for Amazon.com. Though the figures would change, the same principles would apply to setting a U.K. price, if that's your primary market. (In the U.K., though, Amazon currently offers "Super Saver Delivery" on all purchases without minimum.) But with Lightning now distributing to numerous countries in several currencies, with more on the way, how do you work out an ever-growing number of list prices?

Perhaps the most direct approach would be to convert your primary list price into those other currencies, based on current exchange rates. This may have been viable once, but nowadays, volatility in those rates makes it impractical. Also, this approach doesn't take into account higher print costs and resulting higher book prices outside the U.S.

The approach I recommend instead is to peg your list prices to production costs in each currency. This works well because Lightning's print charges are fairly stable, enabling you to set list prices that seldom or never have to be changed (unless, of course, you decide to raise or lower *all* prices of a book).

There are actually three ways (and maybe more) to figure pricing from production costs. Since they all give roughly the same results, you can use whichever feels most comfortable.

1. Figure out a book's pricing multiple in your primary country, then use the same multiple for other currencies. For example, the current $14.00 list price for *Aiming at Amazon* in the U.S. is 3.6 times its production cost of $3.89. Taking its U.K. production cost of £3.00, I would multiply by the same 3.6, giving me a U.K. list price of £10.50.

2. Compare a book's production cost in another country to the cost in your own. That is, derive a ratio from the raw figures, without regard to currency or exchange rate. For example, I would divide *Aiming at Amazon's* U.K. production cost of 3.00 (in GBP) by its U.S. production cost of 3.89 (in USD), giving me a ratio of .77—which I would round off to .75. I would then multiply the $14.00 U.S. list price by that ratio to get the U.K. list price of £10.50.

3. In a variation of #2, calculate the ratio directly from the per-page and unit charges listed in Lightning's operating manuals and contract addendums, without figuring costs of

individual books. Again, this is working with raw figures only. (This is the method I use myself.)

With method #2 or #3, you can use the production cost ratio you've calculated to quickly convert any list price from one currency to the other. In fact, if you're brave, you can use the ratios I've already calculated for myself. (These have been rounded a bit.)*

> U.K./U.S. = .75
> Canada/U.S. = 1.2
> E.U./U.S. = .85
> Australia/U.S. = 1.5

With these ratios, the list prices for *Aiming at Amazon*— with rounding to the nearest half unit—would be

> USD 14.00
> GBP 10.50
> CAD 17.00
> EUR 12.00
> AUD 21.00

Because I'm really lazy, I go one more step toward simplifying my pricing. Instead of figuring and recording each price for each book, I just keep a chart of corresponding list prices for the various currencies. Knowing the U.S. list price, I can then quickly look up any of the others. (It helps that most of my prices are in $2 increments.) Following this section is "Aaron's POD Price Chart," if it helps you.

---

* These ratios are based on figures in the 9/22/2009 Espresso Book Machine Contract Addendum posted on Lightning's Web site. The print charges in that addendum are the same as the charges for regular printing in the U.S. and U.K. operating manuals—plus there are figures for Canada and Australia not found elsewhere.

Note, though, that you may have to fudge a bit with a standardized system of this kind if you've adjusted a primary price for a special purpose. For example, if I raise a U.S. price by $2.00 to catch an Amazon discount or take advantage of Super Saver Shipping, I don't want to carry over that increase to other countries. So, as my base for conversion, I would use the price *before* adjustment.

Obviously, determining list prices by any conversion formula is inferior to the kind of customized pricing we talked about earlier—but if you have a lot of books or are selling in markets unfamiliar to you, it can save your sanity. And that will be even more true as Lightning keeps adding markets.

A final point about pricing when working with Lightning: *Do not print any list price on your book or embed it in your bar code.* Online booksellers don't need that, and neither does any bookstore that special orders. Meanwhile, it can be a nuisance for booksellers *outside* your country.*

But most important, with a price announced on the book, a change of price means a change of book cover. With Lightning, changing a price can be extremely simple—but if you must change your cover too, it can be anything but.

---

* Barnes & Noble requires prices to be printed on the cover and embedded in the bar code—but this is only for books accepted for stocking in B&N stores. It is not required for books that are special ordered by stores or sold by BN.com.

Aaron's POD Price Chart

USD	GBP	CAD	EUR	AUD
$3.00	£2.00	$3.50	€2.50	$4.50
$4.00	£3.00	$5.00	€3.50	$6.00
$6.00	£4.50	$7.00	€5.00	$9.00
$8.00	£6.00	$10.00	€7.00	$12.00
$10.00	£7.50	$12.00	€8.50	$15.00
$12.00	£9.00	$14.00	€10.00	$18.00
$14.00	£10.50	$17.00	€12.00	$21.00
$16.00	£12.00	$19.00	€13.50	$24.00
$18.00	£13.50	$22.00	€15.50	$27.00
$20.00	£15.00	$24.00	€17.00	$30.00

Refuse Returns

In the book business, bookstores are generally allowed to return any book they don't sell—and most of them do. Returns are a bane of traditional publishing, reducing profits, raising prices, and promoting waste. But wholesalers won't even stock your book if it can't be returned.

Unless, again, you're working with Lightning Source. Books distributed by Lightning can be set up with returns allowed or not. Like your discount, this can be set per book and even per country per book.

If you say yes to returns, you will typically get a return rate of a few percentage points—mostly due to customers ordering your book from a bookstore and never picking it up. But in some cases, the rate might be much higher—for instance, if you get media attention for a timely subject, or if your book is ordered by college bookstores for classes.

If you say no to returns, all sales are final, and no book should come back to you. Books may still be returned to Ingram or Lightning if defective, but that should be handled without troubling you. Special orders abandoned by customers will have to be placed on the bookstore shelves for sale. Now, isn't that all better?

Of course, refusing returns will still mean that your book will never be stocked by most stores. But if you've been following my advice, you've already made pretty sure of that.* What's more relevant is that refusing returns of your book will *not* stop any bookseller from special ordering as before.

---

* There was at least one case in which Barnes & Noble for a while seemed to stock a short-discount Lightning book that was returnable. But I know of no recent examples.

Actually, refusing returns is even more desirable with Lightning than in traditional publishing, because they'll cost you quite a bit more. This is true for either option that Lightning offers for how it handles returns.

Under the first plan, all copies are simply destroyed, and you're out the production cost—which is higher than it would be with traditional publishing. Under the second plan, Lightning will send you the copies—but *you* have to pay the shipping cost. You also have to find a market for the returns.*

Obviously, neither plan is good for you. What's more, if you try accepting returns and find you don't like it, changing your policy won't immediately turn them off. Copies sold previously can still be returned for a full six months.

Amazon shows no reluctance to order books that are not returnable. At this writing, Amazon keeps about three weeks' worth of stock of most of my nonreturnable books. At the same time, several other publishers I know who accept returns find that their books, despite healthy Amazon sales, are not stocked there at all—possibly because returnability has led to better stocking at Ingram!

Now, why was it you wanted to accept returns?

---

* Actually, Lightning doesn't send you the returned copies—it destroys them and sends you new ones. So, at least you know the books will be saleable.

6
Preparing Your Files

Caution! Some of this chapter is fairly technical and will benefit from some prior knowledge of book design and graphic arts. It's meant mostly for whoever will be preparing your files for Lightning Source. If that's not you, and if they're not experienced in working with Lightning, it would be a good idea to show this to them.

　　If you need more general help with book design and production, you might see my book *Perfect Pages,* on self publishing with Word 2003 and 2004 or earlier. Brief tips and resource recommendations are in *Aiming at Amazon.*

Prepare Your Pages

In most ways, preparing your book for Lightning Source is the same as preparing your book for a self publishing company—which has to make sense, since nearly all such companies use Lightning for at least some of their printing. But when you're working with Lightning directly, you take that preparation a final step and produce working PDF files.

PDF—*Portable Document Format*—is one of the technological foundations of print on demand. (Don't get caught talking about "PDF format"—that's redundant.) PDF allows documents to display and print on a variety of computers with all content and formatting intact. I'm sure you're familiar with PDF from files you download from the Web. Much of the print industry—and especially the POD industry—uses this same kind of file to guarantee fidelity of the final product to the original design.

It's not absolutely essential that you submit PDF files to Lightning. You can simply print out your book pages centered on standard letter-size or A4 paper—preferably on a laser printer, but otherwise with top-quality paper on an inkjet—then send them to Lightning for scanning. For a reprint, you can even send the book itself. Or, at the other end of the technological scale, you can send source files from Lightning-approved page layout programs like InDesign or QuarkXPress.

But any of these types of submission simply become materials from which Lightning generates PDF files. Lightning encourages you to submit the book yourself in this form—and you certainly gain the greatest quality, convenience, control, and/or flexibility if you do.

The gold standard for generating PDF files is Adobe Acrobat, or more specifically the PDF generator that comes with it,

Acrobat Distiller. There are many other ways to generate PDF files today—cheap or free utilities, export features from word processors or page layout programs, online services, even capabilities built into your computer operating system. The problem is that the files they generate may not work properly or optimally on commercial printing presses, even if those same files display and print perfectly at home.

According to Lightning technicians, even PDF files exported directly by InDesign or QuarkXPress can cause problems—for instance, with transparency, drop shadows, or other vector effects, or with special characters in quirky fonts. And when you use a less capable PDF program or feature, even if files work correctly, you might not get the control over them you need for highest quality output.

That's why Lightning exclusively recommends Distiller for making PDF files. Other methods may work most of the time and for most purposes, but Distiller will give you the highest reliability and enable the highest quality, potentially saving you money, time, hassle, and embarrassment. At the same time, Acrobat provides tools for fixing less-than-optimal PDF files, allowing you to use less professional programs to create your content. For myself, I consider Acrobat an essential part of my toolkit, and I don't leave home without it.

Which version to use? I recommend getting Acrobat Pro in the latest version that will run on your system. An earlier or less powerful version might lack an important feature or not work at all with your current software.

For that reason, most of my discussion will be based on Acrobat 9 Pro, the current version as of this writing. So, you'll need that version or later to make sure it has a feature I describe. (On the other hand, Acrobat 7 and 8 Pro have *most* of the same features—and if it runs on your system, any version back to Acrobat 4 can produce files with acceptable results for black-and-white books and their covers.)

Acrobat offers more than one way to produce PDF files, and even more than one way to create them through Distiller—which is what you want. The specific methods available to you will depend on your versions of Acrobat and other software. But the method you can always count on is to first produce a PostScript file of your document and then process it with Distiller directly.

In most cases, you'll also be able to send documents to Distiller by printing to an "Adobe PDF" print driver. You may even be able to use Distiller via PDFMaker, Acrobat's plug-in for Microsoft Word and other Office programs—but *recent* versions of the plug-in don't use Distiller! When in doubt, create your PDF file, open it in Acrobat or Adobe Reader, and select "Properties" from the File menu. On the Description tab, the PDF Producer should be specified as Acrobat Distiller.

To simplify use, Acrobat Pro offers a number of Distiller profile presets. Lightning recommends using a preset based on and named for a particular printing standard: PDF/X-1a:2001, or just PDF/X-1a, as I'll usually call it here.*

Unfortunately, the PDF/X-1a preset does *not* work with Word for the Mac. You'll get a file that *looks* OK—but when Lightning gets it, your text will print out gray instead of black. † So, Mac Word users should instead first use a Distiller profile like "High Quality" or "High Quality Print" that leaves colors unchanged. You can then go on to convert the file to PDF/X-1a

---

* Strictly speaking, the "2001" is needed for clarity today, because there is a later revision, PDF/X-1a:2003. But I hope I may be excused the lapse, because otherwise, you're going to get very tired of seeing the full name.

† Though Word for Windows outputs black text in grayscale, Word for the Mac outputs it in RGB. With Distiller's PDF/X-1a profile and Lightning's recommended output intent, this becomes CMYK rich black with 90% of the black component—which on a black-and-white press prints as gray.

with Acrobat Pro's Preflight feature. For the profile, choose "Convert to PDF/X-1a (SWOP)." That will convert the color, but in this case correctly. (Be aware, though, due to the way Acrobat handles fonts on OS X, this Preflight conversion takes a Very Long Time.)*

If you prefer to mix and match settings, the essentials are fairly simple and straightforward. Regardless of the Acrobat version you're using, set the compatibility to "Acrobat 4.0 (PDF 1.3)." *All* fonts must be embedded to make sure your text will print as expected, and all should be subset with the percentage of characters setting at 100%.

Adobe's default setting for image compression for commercial printing is "Automatic (JPEG)." This applies JPEG compression to photos, paintings, and other continuous-tone art, and Zip compression to everything else. Though the JPEG image *format* is not the best choice when creating your content, JPEG image *compression,* when applied once in producing your PDF file, should be all right, as long as it's set for maximum quality or minimum compression (two ways of saying the same thing). But if you're a purist and don't have too many images in your book, you might instead choose Zip compression or turn off compression entirely. Just keep in mind that PDF files over 250MB can't be uploaded to Lightning and must be sent on disc instead.

Now that I've made my pitch for Acrobat, let me admit that many Lightning self publishers use cheap or free alternatives and are perfectly happy with the results. To increase your chances of success in this:

---

* Better yet, before converting to PDF/X-1a, use Acrobat Pro's Convert Colors command to convert the file to grayscale. For Conversion Profile, choose "Dot Gain 20%" (without embedding it), and select the option "Preserve Black" or "Preserve Black Objects." With this extra step, your file should be about flawless.

- Stick to fonts from Adobe, Microsoft, and Apple.
- Avoid vector drawings like you might create in Microsoft Word or Visio.
- Don't add special effects like drop shadows, boxes, shading, or transparency.

Also, if you're brave or foolish enough to try Word 2007's PDF export feature on your book, be sure to use the PDF/A option, or some fonts might not get embedded. (But please note that, despite the similarly geeky name, PDF/A is *not* the same as PDF/X-1a, or even close. It's intended for digital archiving, not for commercial printing!)

When producing the PDF file for your book interior, you can choose the document's paper size according to whatever's easiest for you. Lightning lets you either make it the same as your book's trim size or else leave it a standard letter-size or A4 and center your book page on it. Just make sure that each individual page in the PDF file is a separate page in the book, not two facing pages combined. (It's OK if they're *displayed* as facing pages, as long as they can also be separated for viewing or printing.) Don't add crop marks or any other printer marks.

Lightning needs a blank page at the end of your book to print data for its own use in manufacturing, and also to print any legally-required information—but Lightning will take care of all that. If you submit the file with an odd number of pages, Lightning will add just one page for itself. If there's an even number, Lightning will add two. In any case, do *not* add any blank pages yourself.

Due to the way its machinery operates, Lightning also needs your page count to be a multiple of either four or six, depending mostly on trim size but possibly also varying from one printing to the next. To achieve this, additional blank pages are added as needed at press time—but you are not charged for them. (Blank pages at a book's end are common even in offset printing, and there won't be enough extra to throw off your spine width significantly—so don't worry about any of that.)*

What I'm mostly giving here are special considerations when producing files for Lightning rather than another POD provider. Of course, for more details, you should carefully study Lightning's current operating manual plus its various production guides—especially its "File Creation Guide." These guides can be accessed from the File Creation menu on Lightning's site, but only *before* you log in.

---

* If you come across Lightning or anyone else throwing around terms like Mod-2, Mod-4, Mod-6, this is just techie talk for printing pages in multiples.

A Better Reprint

If you want to reprint an older book that's black-and-white, Lightning Source lets you submit a printed copy for scanning. Typically, you might also submit a revised title page and copyright page with updated book info. Lightning then takes those materials and creates a single PDF file for the interior.

While this might produce a book of adequate quality, text and graphics might look a bit rough. Generally, your best bet is to start fresh and produce a new PDF file on your computer. But what if you don't have all the materials you need in a convenient form? Let's look at several scenarios, starting with the simplest.

Scenario #1: You have an all-text book, but you don't have the text in digital form.

Obviously, you could retype the text onto your computer, or hire someone else to type it, but this isn't the most efficient method. A better idea is to use OCR—*optical character recognition*—which scans the page and converts it to digital type.

You can handle this in several ways. Probably the most efficient and cost-effective is to find a document scanning or imaging service that has an OCR option. Or find an OCR specialist who might charge more but possibly give more reliable results.

You can instead do some or all of the work yourself—though if you don't already have the software, this might not cost any less. The simplest way is to scan from within an OCR program and output directly to text. Or you can scan to create images for later processing, following the recommendations in your OCR program documentation.

To avoid drudgery, you might have someone else do the basic scanning before performing OCR yourself. Again, a document scanning service can do this. And so can Lightning itself, if you set up your book at first for "Short Run" only, instead of "Distribution." Lightning will automatically scan at specs well suited to OCR. After you've approved the proof, about another fifty dollars will get Lightning to send you a copy of the PDF file it produced for printing.

Though desktop OCR programs can commonly "read" images in formats like TIFF or JPEG, it's more rare for them to recognize text in image-based PDF files such as you'd get from Lightning. Among those that *can* do that are several from the software company ABBYY—namely, PDF Transformer and FineReader Professional, both for Windows, and FineReader Express Edition for Mac. If you don't find them elsewhere, go to ABBYY's online store, at

www.abbyy.com/shop

If you start with high-quality printed text, your OCR output may need surprisingly little cleanup. Still, you can't count on *any* OCR job to be 100% accurate, so your digital text should be proofread carefully for errors. If you don't do that yourself, an OCR specialist could do it for an extra charge, or you could hire a proofreader separately.

Here's an idea to help with proofing: Perform OCR twice, with two different programs—for instance, have it done by your scanning service but do it again at home. Then use the Compare Documents command in Word. Most of the errors of each program should appear as differences between the two documents.

If you had Lightning do the scanning, submit your new PDF file as a revision of the book. At the same time, ask for "Short Run" to be changed to "Distribution." After that, you'll need to visit the Title Information and Links area on Lightning's Web site, go to your book's page, and "Request Price Change" to set up the individual markets.

Scenario #2: You have a photo-illustrated book with a sophisticated, well-designed layout. You'd rather not lay out the book again from scratch, but you do want the photos to look their best. You still have the original, unscreened photos that were used for the earlier edition.

First get your pages scanned, this time without OCR. In most cases, the scanning should be set for black-and-white "line art"—not grayscale or color—at 600 ppi (pixels per inch), with no lossy compression. Lightning's approach is a bit different, but its PDF files are fine for this purpose anyway.

Next, import the pages into a page layout program. If you have a multi-page PDF file such as Lightning provides, you can import the entire file at once into a recent version of Adobe InDesign. Or you can use Acrobat to convert all pages to separate, numbered files ready for import, either by "extracting" to PDF or by "exporting" to TIFF. You may need to adjust the placement of page images for consistent margins, and some pages may have to be rotated slightly to make them perfectly straight.

Finally, scan the original photos in grayscale and edit as needed in your photo-paint software. You want the photos to end up at the exact size needed, with a resolution of 300 ppi (pixels per inch). Then place the photos on top of the scanned page images, in the same positions as before. Do *not* screen these new photo scans—leave that job to Lightning's printing software.

Scenario #3: You have digital text, but you don't have the original photos. You only have the screened photos as printed in the original book—in other words, photos converted into a grid of tiny black-and-white dots for printing. (Look at them under a magnifier if you're not sure.)

You can't do as well with these, but you can still manage an improvement. Scan just the photos out of the book, but in grayscale and with the scanner software set to automatically *descreen* at the same time. For best results, scan at 300 ppi—no higher!—and for the descreening, specify the line screen that was used for your book.

Don't know what that line screen was? Fancy that. Generally, a setting of 150 lpi (lines per inch) is close enough. Photos on uncoated paper might have a screen of 133, while photos on coated paper might have a screen of 175.

But here's a way to measure the screen of a black-and-white photo exactly, and without special equipment: Set the scanner for black-and-white "line art," choose a resolution around 1200 ppi, and scan one of the photos from your book. Try to choose one with a large area of light gray. Open the scan in a photo-paint program and zoom in. You should clearly see a pattern of dots in different sizes.

Though you might see straight, horizontal rows in this enlargement, line screens are applied and measured diagonally. So, rotate your graphic to a different angle till you again see the dots line up horizontally. If the angle is correct, they will now line up vertically as well.

Now, find that large area of light gray and position it beside the program's vertical ruler on your monitor screen. With the pencil tool, and measuring with that enlarged, on-screen ruler, draw two marks exactly 1 inch apart. Count off the number of rows between those marks, placing additional marks as needed to help keep your place.

The number of rows you count is the measure of the line screen used for your book. You can now go back and scan your photos in grayscale at 300 ppi with descreening at the correct lpi setting, then position them in your new file.

Another way to handle this is, again, to get a scan of the book from Lightning. In Lightning's recent scans, photos are descreened automatically. Starting with the PDF file, you can export individual pages from Acrobat as TIFFs, bring them into your photo-paint program, and crop to the photos.

You may find scenarios different than the ones described here. But by mixing and matching these techniques, you should be able to at least improve your book's quality.

Prepare Your Cover

When preparing your book cover, it's important to understand that Lightning Source has two distinct ways of handling PDF cover files. "Favored" files are passed on for printing just as they are, without additional processing. These covers print with smooth-edged vector type at the full resolution of the press.

Files that are *not* favored are less lucky. With these, Lightning will *rasterize the entire cover*—turn it into a bit-mapped image at a lower resolution—and in the process often *antialias* it as well—make edges appear smoother by adding intermediate colors at the cost of reduced sharpness. That image is then screened when printed, and your type winds up with edges that look either slightly bumpy or slightly fuzzy—at least to someone taking a very close look.

What determines whether your file is favored or not? It's how closely you follow Lightning's recommendations (including any "requirements" that Lightning doesn't actually insist on). These recommendations are designed to produce trouble-free files, and the farther you depart from them, the more likely a Lightning technician will play it safe by rasterizing the whole thing.

Let me make that clear: To avoid any possible trouble, the tech may rasterize your cover *even if you observed all strict requirements and there is nothing actually wrong with it.* Both your cover and your PDF file may have passed rigorous preflight testing on your desktop, but that won't make a bit of difference to Lightning.

For rasterized covers, Lightning does manipulate the type bumpiness to minimize its effect, so most readers don't notice anything objectionable—and you probably wouldn't either, if

I hadn't mentioned it. Still, you'll get a cleaner look if the type is printed as vectors. So, let's take a close look at Lightning's most important recommendations for cover files.

• Use Lightning's custom template. On Lightning's Web site, under the File Creation menu—available only *before* you log in—you'll find a custom cover template generator. This generator is a simple form that asks for trim size, page count, paper color, and so on, then has the template generated and emailed to you with instructions. The page count must be even, so if you have an odd number of pages, round up by one. Note that, depending on how busy Lightning's servers are, the template may take several hours to arrive.

The template itself is a document for import into your cover creation program. For file type, you can choose among InDesign, QuarkXPress, EPS, or PDF. Only fairly recent versions of InDesign and QuarkXPress are officially supported.

Opening the template, you'll see a page of the same size as the sheet of paper on which Lightning will print your cover. On it will be guidelines for placement of all elements of your cover, including spine and bleed. In an InDesign or QuarkX-Press template, these guidelines will be nonprinting, but in an EPS or PDF template, you'll have to remove or cover them before submitting the file.

You'll also see a bar code for your back cover. In an In-Design or QuarkXPress file, you can keep this bar code in view by sending your own cover elements behind it, and you can also move it to a different position, if you prefer. A companion bar code, which you should *not* move, appears for Lightning's use outside the area for the cover.

Any cover that Lightning is to print *must* at some point be placed on one of these templates. You can either do it yourself, or you can let Lightning do it. But if Lightning does it, the tech *will rasterize your cover before placing it on the template.*

Does all this mean you must use the template to build your cover from scratch? No. If you prefer, you can compose your cover separately, convert it to PDF, then place it onto the template, all in one piece. And you'll probably find that easier, especially since Lightning's template places your cover off-center on the sheet. Just make sure your cover fits entirely within the template's guidelines.

• Produce the PDF file with Acrobat Distiller. I've already told you this is Lightning's preference for all files—but for your cover, the tech will actually go to its Document Properties in Acrobat and check the "PDF Producer" specified on the "Description" tab. (You can check it yourself either in that program or in the free Adobe Reader.) If this says "PDF Library," or anything at all besides a version of "Acrobat Distiller," your cover will be rasterized. Period.

That means, for best results, you should *not* use the ultra-convenient PDF export command in your chosen page layout program to produce the file you send to Lightning—no, not even when working in Adobe's own InDesign. That is a clear invitation to rasterization. But if you first compose your cover *off* the template, PDF export is fine for creating the one-piece image you will then place *on* the template.

• Make the file comply to the PDF/X-1a:2001 standard. PDF/X-1a—as I'm calling it here for short—mandates a set of document properties that will ensure trouble-free printing on commercial presses. These include embedding of all fonts, "flattening" of all layers and transparency, conversion of RGB color to CMYK, and stripping out of color profiles. In other words, PDF/X-1a compliance automatically meets many of the requirements Lightning specifies independently, giving you a quick, convenient way to deal with them all. Again, to generate a compliant file, Lightning recommends using Distiller's PDF/X-1a profile preset.

The tech will check for compliance with PDF/X-1a by looking for a notation in Document Properties on the "Custom" tab. (Sorry, this one's in Acrobat only, not in Adobe Reader.) But note that, to achieve this compliance, you don't have to use Distiller's preset as is. Some settings in this preset are crucial to the standard, but others are only defaults. For example, it wouldn't work for you to block the conversion of RGB color to CMYK, but it would be OK to change how images are compressed.

So, it's fine to start with the PDF/X-1a preset, alter it to suit your preferences, and even save it as a custom preset for further use. There's not much danger in experimenting with settings, because if a change conflicts with the standard, Distiller will just refuse to finish the job.

Alternatively, you could start by generating your file with another Distiller profile entirely. You would then "fix" the file with Acrobat Pro's Preflight feature, using its profile "Convert to PDF/X-1a (SWOP)"—as I recommended earlier to make a compliant file from Microsoft Word for the Mac.

Here's another approach that likely will *not* work: Start with a profile other than PDF/X-1a and *add* compliance with settings on the Standards tab. Chances are, you'll just get an error message when you use the profile, because it won't automatically correct problems like the recommended profile will.

As with the requirement to use Distiller, you do *not* have to apply PDF/X-1a to a cover first composed off the template, as long as you apply it to your final file.

If you follow all the recommendations I've discussed, your cover *should* pass through without rasterization. But I won't guarantee it, because it's at the discretion of the individual Lightning tech.

To check for it on your proof, look through a magnifier at the type—especially black type—that was originally vector.

If the cover was rasterized but without antialiasing, you'll see smooth edges on vertical and horizontal strokes but bumps on diagonals and curves. If it was also antialiased, the edges having bumps will be more random, and you'll also see a series of dots running alongside some edges.

You may well decide that preventing rasterization is more trouble than it's worth, if your software doesn't support these requirements. Or you may be planning a bitmapped cover anyway, created in a photo-paint program. In such cases, you can minimize the drawbacks of rasterization by entirely avoiding small or delicate type. Even type that's larger will benefit from using a simple, sturdy font.

Whether or not you use Lightning's template, Lightning will supply a bar code for your cover, so there's no need to add your own—but if you expect your cover to be rasterized, it's especially important *not* to add one. It could easily be ruined by Lightning's antialiasing. In that case, Lightning may replace it anyway, or worse, print the degraded one. Again, check it with a magnifier. You may never hear any complaints about a degraded bar code, but that doesn't mean it won't cause occasional problems.

Lightning asks for all colors to be in CMYK, a color mode supported by professional graphics and page layout programs. It's the native mode of print media, and in that way opposite to RGB, which is used in computer monitors, TVs, and other light emitters. CMYK is named after four colors, namely cyan, magenta, yellow, and black, that are blended to create all others, while RGB is named similarly after red, green, and blue.

RGB color is prohibited by the PDF/X-1a standard, and as I said, that standard's preset has Distiller automatically convert any RGB to CMYK. (Note that this conversion does not touch anything in black and white or in grayscale. Those color modes are compatible with CMYK and fine to use alongside it—and anyway, black, white, and gray are not considered "colors" in this context.) In fact, you can make any Distiller profile do the same with the setting "Convert All Colors to CMYK" on the Color tab.

This means you can feel free to place RGB images in your cover creation program, knowing they'll be converted to CMYK when you produce your PDF file. Such a workflow has become increasingly popular among professionals for its flexibility. Meanwhile, for nonprofessionals, it allows prior image editing in consumer programs like Photoshop Elements that don't support CMYK.

Actually, if you don't care about creating a "favored" file, you can even submit RGB images on your cover *without* conversion. Lightning will then convert them for you during its normal processing. You'll have to accept that the colors may not come out exactly as you wish—but that would be true if you converted them yourself with Distiller. (In either case, you'll get closer fidelity if you practice color management and embed color profiles. Though Lightning warns against such embedding, that should really apply only to elements in CMYK, grayscale, or black and white.)

At this point, you might be wondering why you can't create your whole cover in any old program and leave CMYK conversion to either Distiller or Lightning. It's not quite that simple, though, due mostly to an element you might never suspect as likely to cause complications: black type. You see, in RGB, black is defined simply as 0% of all three color components. (White is 100% of each.) But there's no single definition for CMYK black, and different formulations are used for different purposes and settings.

For fonts in normal text, black for type is usually "pure black," made up of 100% black—a single solid layer—and 0% of all other color components. This produces the cleanest of edges—which is why, for instance, bar codes must *always* be pure black. But for larger type and for graphics, "rich black" is generally preferred, as it blends in other colors for a deeper, warmer tone. Lightning recommends pure black for font sizes below 24 points, and rich black for 24 points and up.

But rich black itself has no single definition. It can range up to 400% total ink coverage—a 100% solid layer of each of the four CMYK components—and this *registration black* is used for alignment marks in offset printing. But for actual print content, that's too much ink for any kind of printing or paper, so it has to be stepped back.

For color offset presses with high-quality paper, the highest acceptable total—the *total ink limit*—is 300%. But for Lightning's cover printing, it's 240%—about the same as for offset printing on newsprint. So, Lightning requires you to stay pretty much within that 240% for the covers you submit. For rich black within that limit, Lightning recommends a composition of 60% cyan, 40% magenta, 40% yellow, and 100% black.*

A professional program like Adobe InDesign, Illustrator, or Photoshop lets you work in CMYK and define the exact color of your type. So, it's no problem to set black type to either pure black or to a rich black that fits within Lightning's limits. The same goes for an intermediate program like Microsoft Publisher, as long as it has CMYK support (as Publisher does in recent versions).† Meanwhile, programs that define black type in grayscale—like Microsoft Word for Windows—don't provide any way to create rich black, but at least their pure black won't cause any trouble on the press.

---

* *Total ink limit* is the technical term whether referring to actual ink or to toner. But with Lightning's covers, *ink* is also literally correct, because they're printed on HP Indigo presses with special oil-based ink.

† When working in CMYK in Microsoft Publisher, you may have to settle for exporting your PDF file directly. If you try to use Distiller from Acrobat 9 Pro, it fouls up your CMYK color definitions.

The big problem comes with programs that define black type in RGB—like Word for the Mac or Photoshop Elements. Converting their black type to CMYK at default settings will typically give you a rich black at 300%—beyond Lightning's limit. To make sure that doesn't happen, you'll need to handle the conversion yourself and *not* do it as Lightning recommends, with the PDF/X-1a Distiller profile. Instead, generate your PDF file with color unchanged, then convert RGB black type to CMYK pure black with Acrobat Pro's Print Production tools.

I've already described one way to do this that will work for a word processor like Word for the Mac: Use the Preflight feature and its profile "Convert to PDF/X-1a (SWOP)." Another way that should work with *any* program is to use the Convert Colors command. For the conversion profile, use "U.S. Web Coated (SWOP) v2," and do *not* choose to embed it. Then select the option "Preserve Black" or "Preserve Black Objects"—which is what protects black type from becoming rich black. Finally, after using either Preflight or Convert Colors, check your results in Output Preview. (When checking, be sure text smoothing is turned *off* in Acrobat Pro's Page Display preferences, or you'll get color values not in the file.)

If RGB conversion seems too complicated, or if you don't have Acrobat Pro, you could use only colored type, and none too dark. Or you could stick with black, avoid thick type, and pray that Lightning accepts the file as is. The 240% limit isn't rigid—if not much of your cover exceeds it, Lightning might let it pass. This too is up to the tech.

By the way, if you're wondering why Lightning discourages color profiles in your PDF files, it's mostly because of black type. If CMYK type has a color profile attached to it, the type may unintentionally be converted during printing from pure black to rich black, or from black to gray. The PDF/X-1a standard has all color profiles stripped out to avoid any chance of this.

Lightning's total ink limit applies not only to type but also to backgrounds and images. For these, your best bet is simply to avoid big blocks of very dark color. But if your heart is set on high contrast, a somber mood, or Goth styling, see "Ink Limits and Images," which follows this section.

One final pitfall in cover creation: POD presses can't use the same cover coatings used in offset. *Any* cover coating will *darken* your colors, and I always lighten my midtones by 10% to compensate. But the glossy lamination that Lightning has to apply will also *warm* your colors slightly. Personally, that hasn't bothered me—but if you're a stickler for color accuracy, it's something to take into account.

I warned you at the beginning of this chapter that it was going to get technical, and that you might need help! If you're willing to tackle it on your own, more power to you.

Ink Limits and Images

As I said in the section on preparing your cover, one of the concerns in commercial printing is making sure not too much ink (or toner) is applied to the paper. Though Lightning Source has long recommended a 240% "total ink limit" for book covers, it's only since 2009 that Lightning has enforced the limit by rejecting covers that significantly exceed it. Such rejections catch many less tech-savvy publishers off guard, and even experienced book designers may not know a good way to deal with it.

So, how do you make sure your book cover is compliant, other than simply by avoiding big blocks of dark color? It's easy enough to change your areas of single color, as we've already discussed in relation to black type—at least, it is with professional programs like Adobe Photoshop, InDesign, Illustrator, or Acrobat Pro. But what if darker colors are all mixed into a continuous-tone graphic like a photo or a scanned painting?

Lightning has issued a recommended procedure for handling this in Photoshop (*not* Photoshop Elements). Unfortunately, as the instructions delicately put it, "there will be visible color changes." This is because the procedure is based on a legacy feature from Photoshop 2—not CS2, but just 2! Really, what's needed is for Lightning to develop a dedicated color profile to manage conversion—but Lightning remains committed to discouraging color management entirely. In fact, the whole problem arises because Lightning expects us to prepare files to a print standard—U.S. Web Coated (SWOP) v2—that is built around coverages up to 300%!

With some experimenting, I've modified Lightning's technique and settings so images that need fixing should stay close to their original colors—at least close enough to require minimal adjustment. It's not perfect, but it may be the best we can do. Again, this is for adjustment of continuous-tone images in Photoshop. (I'm using Photoshop CS4.)

1. Open your image in Photoshop. Preferably, this will be your original RGB image before it was ever converted to CMYK.

2. Go to Edit > Convert to Profile, or in older versions, to Image > Mode > Convert to Profile. Under Conversion Options, use these settings:

> Engine: Adobe (ACE)
> Intent: Relative Colorimetric
> Use Black Point Compensation: Yes
> Use Dither: Yes

3. For the destination space profile, choose "Custom CMYK." If you get a warning about color management, click "OK." Then, in the new dialog box, enter these settings.

> Ink Colors: SWOP (Newsprint)
> Dot Gain: 25%
> Separation Type: GCR
> Black Generation: Medium
> Black Ink Limit: 100%
> Total Ink Limit: 238%
> UCA Amount: 0%

Note that Total Ink Limit is set to 238% instead of 240%. This is to allow for a rounding error during conversion that could push black just over the 240% limit. Though not really a problem in itself, there's no need to have that show up on Lightning's radar.

4. Click "OK" to exit each dialog box and complete the command. Your colors should now all fit within the 240% total ink limit—but you're not quite done.

5. What's left is to move the image back into the standard CMYK space Lightning wants, but *without* changing the ink coverage. Go to Edit > Assign Profile, or to Image > Mode > Assign Profile in older versions—not *Convert to* Profile, which would put you right back where you started! For profile, choose "U.S. Web Coated (SWOP) v2" from the pull-down menu—or you can just click the button for "Working CMYK" if it specifies that profile. Then click OK.

Alternatively for this step, you can use Assign Profile to choose "Don't Color Manage This Document," which will leave the image without any color profile. This should work just as well within any program with color settings for a working CMYK of U.S. Web Coated (SWOP) v2.

Don't see much difference in color from when you started? That's what you want! There will be a slight loss of contrast, and hopefully that's about all. But what should be very different are the ink percentages. Check your darkest areas to make sure they're still under the limits. And if the image no longer looks quite right? Go ahead and adjust it. Just make sure you don't push your colors past the ink limit again!

If you like, you can use Photoshop's soft proofing to check the image and adjust it *before* the profile assignment or removal in that final step. In a custom proof setup, choose "U.S. Web Coated (SWOP) v2" as the device to simulate, and check "Preserve CMYK Numbers."

If you expect to go through this procedure more than a time or two, you can simplify it by using a custom color profile with the settings from step 3. In fact, I've already created one for you, by saving custom CMYK settings from Photoshop's Color Settings dialog. You can download the profile here:

www.newselfpublishing.com/TotalInkLimit.zip

Double-click the file to unzip it, then install the profile in a location checked by Photoshop. (How and where to do that will differ according to your software.) You might need to restart Photoshop before you can see the new profile. From then on, for the destination space profile in step 3, choose "Lightning Source Cover CMYK (238%)"—or whatever I'm calling the current version of my profile—instead of "Custom CMYK."

This color profile can be used in other ways as well—for instance, with the Convert Colors command in Acrobat Pro. By selecting it as the conversion profile (and not embedding it), you can bring an entire PDF file within the 240% limit—type, images, background, and all. Or use it along with that command's selection criteria (introduced in Acrobat 9 Pro) to affect specific elements only. It could help, for example, when converting black type from RGB to CMYK. On a first pass, convert small type to pure black with the "Preserve Black" option, then use this profile to convert larger type to rich black at 240%.

Cope with Color

Color POD is in an even earlier stage of development than is black-and-white POD. With any luck, the advice in this section will be outdated before long. Because frankly, Lightning's requirements for color books are about as quirky as they come.

To simplify things for itself, Lightning has one requirement that can make color POD either easier for you or harder: All interior and cover PDF files, with no exceptions, must conform to the PDF/X-1a:2001 standard. So, if you do not have at least one professional program that can output or convert a PDF file to that standard, you can forget about producing files for color books with Lightning.

Unlike in black-and-white interiors, Lightning *does* honor bleed in color books—but instead of the more common eighth inch, you *must* use a full quarter.* Also, the bleed must be only on the three outside edges of the page. Finally, when you center the bleeded pages on the document paper, the centering must include the area of the lopsided bleed. In other words, the left-hand page trim—the page minus the bleed—will be positioned one-eighth inch right of center to allow for that bleed, while the right-hand page trim will be one-eighth inch *left* of center. (If your book has no bleed, you can just center normally or produce your PDF file at trim size.)

If you're used to providing only the symmetrical pages of black-and-white POD, this "off-centering" may seem a challenge—but you can do it simply in a professional page layout program. In InDesign CS4, for example, when creating your

---

* At this writing, Lightning's "Color Book Addendum" to its U.S. operating manual specifies an eighth-inch bleed—but all other Lightning documentation says otherwise.

document, choose the "Facing Pages" option, then click the "More Options" button and set your bleed. (You can also set or change these later with "Document Setup" on the File menu.) Now, when you produce your PDF file, each page will automatically have both the three-sided bleed and the off-centering required by Lightning.

The final inconvenience that Lightning imposes on you is to restrict you from placing your image closer than one-eighth (.125) inch to the gutter if your color book is perfectbound. This is because ink at the inside edge would weaken the glued binding. (There's no such restriction for saddle-stitched books.)

Personally, I try to design my books so I can produce files to the specifications of *any* POD provider with minimal adjustment. Lightning is the *only* provider that asks me to keep images away from the gutter, so I'm not about to start moving them around for that.

InDesign, though, makes it possible to meet Lightning's requirement *without* moving the image. After positioning it with one edge against the gutter, simply grab the selection handle on that edge and move it one-eighth inch inward. The image itself should be untouched, but an eighth-inch strip of it will be hidden and won't print, leaving the required margin. To restore that strip anytime later, just move the edge back.

If you have an image that *crosses* the gutter, you're out of luck. To use the trick I just described, you'll have to divide the image in your image editor and place one section on each page. And no, Lightning will *not* let you just position a strip of white over the part of the image in the forbidden zone. And yes, I did try that myself!

7
Launching Your Book

Upload to Lightning

Your first stop in launching your book is the Lightning Source Web site and its New Title Setup form. Some of the required info will be used by Lightning alone, while some will be sent on to Ingram, Baker & Taylor, Amazon, Barnes & Noble, and others. Supplying this info shouldn't be difficult if you took my advice about gathering it in one place—you did do that, didn't you?—but navigating Lightning's form itself might be tricky. The main thing to remember is to click on "Save" to finish with one page and move on to the next.

If you want to use a different publishing name on the book than the main one on your account, Lightning will let you choose it as the "imprint." But for the form to offer that name as a choice, you'll have to set it up ahead of time with your Client Services Rep.

In *Aiming at Amazon,* I suggested composing a long subtitle for Amazon but a shorter one for anywhere the long one wouldn't fit. If you're doing that, be sure to give Lightning the short one. Though Lightning's form will accept a longer subtitle, anything much beyond 100 characters will be truncated when it gets to Ingram or Baker & Taylor. (OK, if you want the exact character counts, they're 116 for Ingram and 113 for Baker & Taylor. That's for the subtitle *only.*)*

With names of authors and other contributors, the Lightning/Ingram software can get confused about word order if you include a period—say, for an initial or for an abbreviated title. In fact, if you do that for more than one contributor to a book, you can get parts of one name mixed with another. It's

---

* For instructions on how to substitute the long subtitle for the short one on Amazon, see *Aiming at Amazon.*

best, then, to just leave out the period. The name will still be readable, and punctuation is ignored in search.

For publication date, enter the date you're submitting your files, or one before, or one within a few days after. For street date, just ignore. (For reminders of why, see my earlier section on pub dates.)

The book description you give to Lightning can be up to 4,000 characters—but normal paragraph breaks will be ignored. The only way to separate your text into separate paragraphs—despite Lightning's warning against using HTML—is to place an HTML paragraph start tag (<p>) at the beginning of each new paragraph. If you like, you can also add paragraph end tags, or blank lines between paragraphs, but they're not needed. (Yes, I know that's not correct HTML.) This is how it would look.

> This is a paragraph.
> <p>This is another paragraph.
> <p>This is the final paragraph.

If you don't want to mess with tags, you can just submit a one-paragraph description. But note that the description is one of those pieces of information that can wind up at Amazon and other online booksellers. If you can get it the way you want it here, you won't have to deal with the much chancier methods of submission that Amazon and the others offer.

The page count you give must include *all* pages, whether numbered or unnumbered in your book. Also, the count must be an even number, so if your file has an odd number of pages, round up by one. Do *not* add a blank page to your file to make it match the count—let Lightning do that for you, or you might wind up with another two blank pages on top of that.

Lightning will ask if you want to pay to be listed in *Ingram Advance,* a monthly catalog that features new and upcoming books. This catalog includes a special section, way in the back, where Lightning books are quarantined with a sign stuck on their rear end saying, "IGNORE ME." I have never heard any Lightning publisher claim they've benefited from being listed. (Come to think of it, I've never heard any claims of benefit from anyone at Lightning, either.) While Lightning is mostly free of the kinds of snares set for innocent self publishers at self publishing companies, this apparent imposition by Ingram is the one exception.

One thing Lightning offers that you *do* want is to have a *proof* of the book sent to you. This is a printed copy you check to make sure it came out OK. It's seldom a good idea to approve a book without seeing it, and that's especially true when you're new to publishing, to POD, or just to Lightning. In fact, for your first book, Lightning will insist on sending one. (If you need any more good reasons to get the proof, see "Avoiding a Proof" following this section.)

You will be given a choice of several means of submitting your book. In most cases, uploading your files right then to the Web site is the most convenient, as long as each of your files is under the 250MB limit. A handy progress bar will tell you how far along you are in what can be a lengthy process.

The file upload pages will open in front of the page they're linked from. When you're through uploading, you must return to that earlier page and follow a different link to complete the order for delivery of your proof. (But if you get confused and foul that up, you should get another chance to have the proof sent to you when your rep lets you know she has it in hand.)

The title submission process is fairly long and involved, but if you're interrupted, don't worry. The site will keep the info from whatever pages you've saved, so you can return and pick up where you left off. You'll find a link for that when you log in, on your "My Lightning Account at a Glance" page.

For uploaded files, Lightning will normally take a week or less to process the book and get you a proof—and it can be as little as two days! You can follow your book's progress on the Web site under "Title Information and Links." You don't need to fill in any search criteria—just hit "Start Search," and Lightning will show any titles of yours and their current status.

Click on the status listing—not the book title—to bring up a progress log with dates and times. The specific terms may vary over time, but here is an example of steps to watch for.

Title Submitted, Awaiting Materials
Title in Premedia
BOOKBLK Accepted
COVER Accepted
Proof has been generated
Proof Out

Note that the first entry appears automatically when you submit the book, but all the rest are the result of someone at Lightning manually recording the completion of a step. For instance, your book will show "Awaiting Materials" till your Client Services Rep logs in the files you've uploaded, forwards them for review and processing, and reports that to the system. So, if you upload at night or on a weekend, don't even look for the next step till the start of the next business day.

Returning to the title list, you can get more info on the book by clicking on its title. This calls up a page showing all the info you entered and letting you request changes if something is wrong.

Once your cover is processed, this page will also show the cover image Lightning will send out to Ingram and indirectly to retailers, including Amazon. There's usually nothing wrong with Lightning's image, but sometimes the color can be off.

(The image may also be squeezed out of shape, but ignore that—it's a fault of the Web page coding, not the image.)

If there's a problem with the cover image, you can ask your rep to have it redone, though the results may be the same. You can also ask your rep to replace Lightning's image with one you supply. Or you might find it more convenient to replace it farther down the line, at some of the image's destination sites. Just be aware that Lightning will generate a new image and send it out again any time you submit a new cover file.

On the other hand, if you don't have a cover image of your own, you can use Lightning's. Click on "Zoom" to get the full-size image, then right-click (Windows) or Ctrl-click (Mac) to download it to your computer.

At last you'll have the proof in your hands! If it turns out fine, you'll approve it on the Web site, using a link on the first page after you log in. If you discover any problems with one of your files, you can reject the proof, revise the file, and upload again. Note, though, that you'll be charged each time for processing. So, it's best to check carefully *before* you submit.

Of course, a problem with Lightning's proof might be Lightning's fault and not your own—though this is not common, apart from production glitches affecting individual copies. If you do see a physical problem you're not sure is limited to that one proof copy, you can probably get another copy from Lightning at no added cost—but if you don't expect to be charged, discuss this with your rep.

Keep in mind that Lightning claims the right to a certain tolerance on all measurements on any printed copy—a sixteenth inch in the U.S. In practice, an eighth inch is not uncommon. If you require a closer tolerance, then print on demand is probably not for you.

Once you approve your proof, you'll have to pay for any further corrections, regardless of who made the error. So, do take some time to check your proof carefully.

After approval, you can return to "Title Information and Links" and check the progress log for the final steps.

> Publisher Accepted Proof
> Available for Distribution
> Available for Printing/Download

When you see "Available for Printing/Download," your book is ready to roll.

If you've moved your book to Lightning from a self publishing company or from Amazon Advantage, you may have important steps to perform elsewhere. See the special section "Moving to Lightning" at the end of this chapter.

Avoiding a Proof

Many self publishers will go to almost any lengths to avoid ordering a proof from Lightning. Given the high cost of Lightning's proofs, I can understand this—but personally, I consider it a false economy.

Here are some of the measures tried, and why I think they're bad ideas.

• Do without a proof. Lightning allows this after your first book, but this is a *really* bad idea—especially for a new self publisher. There's always a chance for errors, and even if *you* don't make any, *Lightning* might. For instance, when receiving a revised file, Lightning has been known to neglect to replace the old one. And remember, if you approve a proof without seeing it, any later changes are on your dime, no matter who's at fault.

• Order a proof from another provider. For example, some Lightning publishers order proofs from Lulu.com, using a publishing plan that does not include distribution. (Books with distribution are handled by Lightning, which would create a fatal conflict.) This might be valuable if you're just starting out and want an initial look at your book before sending it to Lightning. But you'll still need a proof from Lightning, because its software and presses may handle your files differently, and you'll need to check for errors by Lightning itself. Also, you should be aware that Lulu has been known to "helpfully" list even nondistributed books on Amazon Marketplace.

• Approve the proof unseen and order a normal copy from Lightning with a less expensive shipping option. I tried this once myself and found that the savings just weren't that much. Also, Lightning books are now listed on Amazon so quickly that faulty copies could be selling before you even receive one yourself. You could avoid that by first setting up the book only for publisher direct ordering then adding whole-sale ordering when you've seen the book. But this can cause availability glitches as well as a loss of sales from the delay.

• Approve the proof unseen and order a normal copy from Amazon. You might save a little more money this way, but you also stand a greater risk of bad copies making it into the wild.

My advice: Just order the proof.

Submit Your Listings

As soon as your files are uploaded at Lightning Source, it's time to submit your title to the independent listing services run by R. R. Bowker and Nielsen BookData, where you set yourself up earlier. And as soon as you approve your proof, you'll want the book listed also by the U.S. wholesaler Baker & Taylor.

Again, the address for Bowker's Identifier Services and your My Identifiers account is

www.myidentifiers.com

(If you're instead using BowkerLink, see "Working with BowkerLink" in the appendix.)

On login, you should see a listing of your ISBNs and any associated book info. If not, click the My Identifiers tab, then "ISBN." Then, on the row of the ISBN you've chosen for your book, click the "View/Edit" button.

You'll be presented with a book info form on a series of tabs. Click from one tab to the other to enter your info. When you're done—not before—click any one of the "Save Changes" buttons that appear at the tab bottoms. (After that, if you need to, you can make more changes and save again.) Your submission will normally be processed within a day, though the Web site says to allow several.

Here are a few more tips to make this form as painless as possible.

• Only some fields are required, as marked.

• Start from the top of each tabbed section and work down. Skipping around on the page may confuse the interactive form.

• If you've given your book both long and short subtitles, use the long one here. Bowker will accept a subtitle that's just as long as the one you give Amazon. (Longer, in fact.)

• Don't list contributors who are not shown on the title page of your book. For instance, if you hired a freelance editor, do *not* list him or her as "Editor."

• For "Title Status," say "Active Record."

• For "Publication Date," provide the same date you gave to Lightning—not the date you're giving to reviewers, if that differs. (You can switch it later, if you like, once both dates have passed.)

• In most cases, "Target Audience" would be "Trade."

• For "Price Type," say "Retail Price."

• The U.S. distributor would be Lightning Source. (It should appear here as an option if you previously sent it to Bowker, as I advised before—but it may take some time after that to show up, because the info must be processed manually.)

• Typically, a Lightning book should be listed at Bowker with U.K. info too—so click "Add Country," select "United Kingdom," and enter price info in British pounds, with Lightning Source UK as the distributor.

• At this writing, Lightning is based in the U.S. and the U.K. only—so don't add other countries unless you live and sell there yourself.

• For copyright year, enter the year printed in your book, whether or not it matches the publication date you gave.

If you can't submit your cover image through your My Identifiers account, wait a day or two after submitting your book info, then email the image to

BowkerLink.Covers@bowker.com

Or for 10 or more, send them on disc to

R. R. Bowker
Attn: Data Services—Images
630 Central Avenue
New Providence, NJ 07974

Images are processed once a week. New images will appear online right after that, while replacements can take a couple more days.

As I said before, Amazon in its early days drew book data automatically from Bowker for its listings, and later it used Bowker as needed to manually verify book data—but neither is true any longer. Nothing you submit to Bowker will automatically show up on Amazon or even be visible to it. More specifically, you *cannot* use an early entry in Books in Print to make Amazon prelist your book.

BN.com, on the other hand, does draw from Bowker. A book you list there should appear on BN.com within a couple of days.

Your next stop is Nielsen BookData's PubWeb. The address, again, is

www.nielsenbookdata.com/pubweb

Here you'll either list your book or—if you already submitted tentative info to get your ISBNs—update and add to the listing.

If you're listing your book fresh, don't put this off. Lightning UK will send data for your book to Nielsen as soon as you approve your proof, and if Nielsen processes that data before yours, Lightning will "own" the listing for that book. And many wholesalers and retailers, including Amazon.co.uk, get their primary data from Nielsen.

PubWeb's form is fairly straightforward. Some tips:

• As in Bowker's forms, many of the fields are not required.

• You will be submitting *only* U.K. sales info. Unlike Bowker, Nielsen does not list for multiple national markets.

• For "Tax Rate," choose "Zero." (That's the U.K tax rate for books, as opposed to other types of product.)

• For "Publication Date," provide the same date you gave Lightning—not the date you're giving to reviewers, if that differs. (You can later switch it, if you like, once both dates have passed.)

• Use your long subtitle, if you have one.

• For "Territorial Rights Information"—assuming you have not sold any rights—you'd normally specify "Exclusive" next to "Worldwide," ignoring the regional choices.

After submitting your data, you can upload your cover image by returning to the initial search form and hitting "Add Jacket." Or you can send it as an email attachment to

Images.Book@nielsen.com

Your image will be sent to numerous wholesalers and on-line booksellers, including Amazon.co.uk, from where it will spread to all Amazon sites worldwide. Nielsen, then, can be used to place or replace any Amazon cover image—but it might not work to give Nielsen an image thoroughly optimized for Amazon.

Nielsen may take a week or two to process your submission. The process is more manual than at Bowker and therefore more prone to error, so you do need to check the results. To find your book from the search form, just leave everything blank and hit "Search."

Note that you will not be able to revise your entry online while waiting for it to post. But if you have any urgent changes, you can send them by email. Price, availability, and publication date changes would go to

TradeData.Book@nielsen.com

Other data would go to

PubHelp.Book@nielsen.com

Later, you can make most changes online, but some—like pub date—may still require an email to that first address.

Unlike with Bowker and Amazon.com, you *can* use an early entry at Nielsen to get prelisted on Amazon.co.uk and other Amazon sites outside the U.S., as well as on the sites of major U.K. chains. But there's generally no great advantage to this, so I don't recommend it.

Baker & Taylor reportedly receives monthly batches of book info from Lightning. But unlike Ingram, B&T does not *list* all the books. Instead, B&T seems to list a Lightning book only when it observes or predicts demand for it. Of course, it's much less likely to see demand for a book it doesn't list!

Luckily, there's a way to make sure Baker & Taylor lists your book. You can do this by submitting the info yourself, using B&T's Vendor Title Submission Form. Find it at

edi.btol.com/publishersubmissions

Generally, the time to do this is right after you approve your Lightning proof. Though the form is basically meant for direct B&T suppliers, it works for Lightning publishers as well, if you're careful how you fill it out.

• If you have subtitles of different lengths, supply your *shorter* one—the same one you gave Lightning.

• For "Publication Date," provide the same date you gave Lightning.

• For "Report Code," say "Available."

• Ignore "Net Price."

- For "Vendor Name," give Lightning Source.
- For "Imprint Name," give your publishing name (or the imprint you're using for the book, if that's different).
- For "Discount to B&T," give the wholesale discount you set at Lightning.

The form doesn't ask whether you accept returns, because publishers listed by B&T are normally required to. But since Lightning publishers are a special case, you should get an email asking whether you do or not. Say yes or no, depending on what you told Lightning. (Don't worry, saying yes does *not* mean you'll get returns directly from B&T.)

If you have ten or more books to list, you can get an Excel submission template and instructions by writing to

BTTitles@btol.com

Listings seem to take about a week to show up in B&T's catalog. I'll tell you later how to check this, as well as how to then add a cover image.

Are you wondering if you can use Baker & Taylor to prelist your book on Amazon? The answer is no—because B&T won't include a book in its feed to retailers unless it's in stock.

If you signed up with your national reproduction rights organization and/or your public lending rights agency—as I recommended in the chapter on becoming a publisher—you might also want to go list your book there. This is especially helpful if it's by an author other than yourself or is under an imprint that's different from your primary publishing name. At CCC's Rights Central, get instructions by clicking the Manage Titles tab, then "Update or Add Titles."

rightscentral.copyright.com

By the way, not all your listings *must* wait till you've uploaded your files. I suggest this timing because, until your book is done, its info may keep changing—and there's no significant advantage to an early listing. But you can submit to Bowker and Nielsen anytime earlier, then go back to make corrections.

Check In on Wholesalers

Once you approve your proof at Lightning Source, basic info on your book is sent automatically to all its direct customers. This includes major booksellers like Amazon and Barnes & Noble. But most booksellers, online or off, will have access to your book and its listing only indirectly, through the wholesalers that Lightning deals with. And even Amazon and B&N will depend on wholesaler listings for details and availability status.

For most U.S. booksellers—including Amazon.com and B&N—the most important wholesaler that will list your book is Ingram Book Company. Unfortunately, Ingram is not as efficient as Lightning. Your *later* books will normally be listed on Ingram's ipage and be available for sale within a week of your proof approval—but your *first* book can take two to four weeks, as Ingram sets you up as a new publisher in its system.

Hopefully, you've already had Lightning set up an account for you on ipage as I suggested. This is the same site used by Ingram customers, and it also reflects the data sent electronically to many of them, including Amazon.com. So, it's important to check your book's listing there. The address again:

ipage.ingrambook.com

After logging in, use the search form to call up your book. If you have more than one book of yours to look up, you can see them all by searching on your publisher prefix as "ISBN."

Note that, for most kinds of searches, the account Lightning gave you lets you access only the "Ingram Active" database—in other words, books for which Ingram is currently accepting orders. This includes books forthcoming or temporarily out of stock, but it does *not* include books out of print or simply not available from Ingram. You can find those, though, with an ISBN search, which automatically accesses "Ingram Extended"—all listed books, available or not. So, if your book has an availability problem, an ISBN search may be the *only* way to check the listing.

From search results, you can click on the book's title to reach its detail page. If you see an error in your book's listing, go back and check whether it originates in data at Lightning, and if so, correct it there. If the error originates at Ingram, you can submit a correction request by using the link that ipage provides at the bottom of the book's detail page, or by emailing the correction to

TQData@ingrambook.com

If there's a problem with the book's availability, you'll see a notice both in search results and on the detail page. If each gives you a different story, the detail page is more current.

The book's detail page shows the price you set at Lightning—the "SRP," suggested retail price—and the base discount that Ingram offers to retailers for your book. This is *not* the "wholesale" discount you set at Lightning, which is what *Ingram* gets. Instead, it's that discount *minus* what Ingram takes for its own cut.

A notation here of "REG, " short for "Regular," means a standard 40% discount, which is what Ingram offers if your discount at Lightning is 55%. "NET" means no discount, for when your Lightning discount is 20% to 25%. If Ingram gives 35%—a standard discount but on the low end, resulting from a Lightning discount of 50%—a "GreenLight" notice appears on both the detail page and in search results. (Sorry, I have no idea why they made it green.)

At top right of the detail page, you'll see figures for copies in stock and copies on order. These are listed for Ingram's distribution centers in Tennessee, Pennsylvania, Oregon, and Indiana. The figures are updated only nightly—with Friday's figures not appearing till Sunday night—but you can see up-to-the-minute figures by clicking on "Real Time Stock Check."

Lightning books are most likely to show stock at the Tennessee distribution center, which is across the street from Lightning's primary U.S. facility. As your book begins to sell, you may also see it stocked at the Oregon center, the closest to Amazon's base of operations. If there's general demand from bookstores, you may see it at other centers as well.

Before you get all excited by the large number of copies you see stocked in Tennessee, let me explain that this number reflects "virtual stocking" of Lightning books. All those books are shown on ipage as having a minimum of 100 copies in stock in Tennessee, but the first hundred is imaginary. The number of copies *really* in stock there is the number *over* 100—which in most cases is zero. (The other warehouses show real figures.)

No, Ingram is not being dishonest. This was Ingram's solution—and a very good one—to a sticky problem with POD books. The whole idea behind print on demand is that books can be readily available *without* being in stock. The original plan for Lightning was that booksellers would *backorder*—the term for ordering a book that isn't in stock but is on its way or at least can be obtained—and that Lightning would quickly produce it and deliver it to Ingram.

But booksellers can be reluctant to backorder, because they normally can't tell when or even *if* a book will arrive. In fact, some booksellers—including all Borders stores—have a *policy* against backordering. So, a Borders special orders clerk might see a Lightning book listed at Ingram but would still not be able to obtain it, even when clearly marked POD.

Even worse for Lightning publishers, Amazon's availability listings make no special allowance for print on demand.

Lightning books not in stock at Ingram were routinely noted as shipping in 3 to 4 weeks or worse, even when the book could really be delivered to Amazon within two weeks. Not good for sales!

Actually, the situation was a good deal more maddening than I've described or than you probably want to know, but all of it was dealt with nicely by virtual stocking. With 100 imaginary copies at Ingram Tennessee, everyone acts as if Lightning's books were always available—which they are—and the whole system runs smoothly. Just like print on demand was supposed to.

Unless you're tinkering with your book at Lightning and it has been temporarily removed from distribution, it should *always* show this virtual stocking on ipage, from shortly after the listing appears. If you don't see it within one business day or so, then Ingram has not properly associated your book with Lightning and doesn't know where to get it. This is unusual but can happen if Ingram already has info on your book before Lightning sends it. Contact Ingram and your Lightning Client Services Rep to correct this problem immediately.

By the way, Ingram is most likely to *actually* stock your book if you're allowing returns. But this provides no substantial advantage to you. In fact, if Ingram is stocking the book well, this just makes Amazon less likely to do so, because drop shipping from Ingram will seem more reliable.

What I've described here is what you can see and do with an ipage *bookseller* account at the "Essential" level—the only kind of account Lightning sets up for new publishers. If you're lucky enough to have gotten a *publisher* account while they were still available, you'll have access to additional info and capabilities, though you'll be missing others. For details, see "iPage Publisher Accounts" in the appendix.

If you don't like the cover image that Lightning created, and you don't want to replace it at Lightning itself—and you know how to upload files by FTP—you may be able to submit a replacement directly to ipage. Request an FTP account from

Andy.Stone@ingrambook.com

Or if Andy's no longer there, write to the email address given earlier and ask for the current contact.

Images uploaded by FTP are posted on ipage. They should also be sent to numerous online booksellers, including Amazon.com—but I haven't seen my own uploads appear anywhere else. (You might have more luck if you haven't replaced your book's image on other sites in other ways.) Also, note that any new cover image generated at Lightning will replace the one submitted here—so you may have to repeat your upload.

While most U.S. booksellers rely on Ingram as their primary wholesaler, others—including Borders and Borders.com—lean more on Baker & Taylor. B&T is also the primary data source for Muze, a third-party catalog content compiler that supplies book data to numerous U.S. businesses online and off, including Buy.com, eBay, Half.com, and Biblio.com.

As I've said, Baker & Taylor doesn't give Lightning publishers direct access to its catalog, but you can check it if you're subscribed to Publisher Alley. That address again is

www.puballey.com

Your listing should be seen on Publisher Alley about a week after you submit it to B&T with the method I described earlier. After signing in, click on "Sales Reports," then on "All Titles." For "Imprint," select "All," then fill in just enough of the rest of the form to get what you need. (There's no way here to see all your books by searching on your ISBN publisher prefix, though you can save a search that includes the ISBNs of all your published books.) From the search results, click on the book's ISBN to see its detail page.

If you see an error in the listing, you can report it by clicking on "Title Feedback" on the detail page. Or email your correction to

DataFix@btol.com

Price corrections, though, go to

PC@btol.com

Contrary to what you'd want to see almost anywhere else, your book's publisher should be listed here on the detail page as "Lightning Source," though with an additional code to identify you. For instance, here's how it should look for *POD for Profit.*

Lightning Source (LGTNR-SHPRD)

That compound code tells B&T that Shepard Publications is the publisher but the book needs to be ordered from Lightning.

If B&T has a cover image for your book, it will appear at top right of the detail page. You can submit an image yourself by sending it as an email attachment to

CoverImages@btol.com

Or if you have a large number of image files to upload, you can use this same address to request FTP access. An image sent to B&T will show up on the sites of many online booksellers—but not on Amazon.

Publisher Alley will also show you B&T's stocking and sales of your book. Summary figures can be seen right in search results. For stocking, you'll see copies on hand ("O/H") and copies on order ("O/O"). For sales, you'll see copies sold, copies returned, backorders—in other words, copies ordered but delayed till B&T receives stock (from Lightning)—and *demand*—which to B&T means the number of copies ordered, whether or not some orders were delayed or cancelled. On the book's detail page, you'll see the same figures broken down by month and/or regional warehouse.

Keep in mind that you're unlikely to see copies of your book on hand. B&T used to stock better-selling Lightning books—but at this writing, it prefers to just list the books and obtain copies as needed to fill backorders.

If you're not subscribed to Publisher Alley, you'll want to find another way to check your book's B&T listing, though you'll still send corrections and images to the email addresses above. One way to check would be to get help from a bookseller or publisher who does have access to B&T's site or to its electronic feed. And another would be to call a B&T sales rep at

800-775-1100

You might have to ask the rep specifically to check national listings, including books tagged as print on demand.

There are indirect ways as well. Half.com will list your book if and only if it's listed by B&T—and once that happens, your book will appear on that site almost at once. The same thing will happen on Borders.com, if you're offering a standard discount.

www.half.com
www.borders.com

Be careful about listings on these sites, though. Since both draw on other sources for extra content, you can't be sure that what they display is exactly what B&T is sending out.

In the United Kingdom, the wholesalers most relied on by Amazon and other booksellers are Gardners Books and Bertrams|THE (formerly Bertram Books). Both list all Lightning books as "Print on Demand" and may also stock the more popular ones. Keep in mind, though, that Amazon.co.uk most often orders direct from Lightning and gets your book info mostly from there and from Nielsen BookData—and that these sources are also the likely origins for errors at the wholesalers themselves.

Bertrams requires no account for you to see details of your book's listing! Find this wholesaler at

www.bertrams.com/BertWeb

But note that, without an account, you can search *only* on ISBN—the other options are there, they just don't work!

Bertrams lists the email address for its current contact for "bibliographic data," but that contact is likely to tell you that any error originates elsewhere. She may even try to notify Lightning UK to correct it—which could cause serious complications. So, I suggest you leave this alone.

Gardners *does* require an account to see full details on your book, and that's not available to Lightning publishers— but in its public area, you can at least see a basic listing. (Don't worry about not seeing the "Print on Demand" notice, because it's shown only in the full listing.)

Find Gardners at

www.gardners.com

You can try sending corrections to

Marketing@gardners.com

But here too, you will probably told it's not their error.

Check In on Amazon

In almost every case, your most important listing will be on Amazon's U.S. store, Amazon.com. Some of your book info will arrive there from Lightning Source and some from Ingram, while some you'll supply yourself.

Appearance of your listing should be automatic once you approve your proof at Lightning Source. But it doesn't happen immediately or all at once! Though Amazon's exact procedures may vary over time, here's what has to happen before the listing is fully established.

• Amazon collects book data from Lightning. This includes the most basic info on your book, including ISBN, title, author, and publisher. This normally occurs overnight after you approve your proof.

• Amazon collects additional book data from Ingram. This may include items such as the book description and the cover image that Ingram received from Lightning. This normally occurs overnight after the book appears on Ingram's ipage.

• The data from each of these sources is integrated by Amazon into its Book Catalog. This allows the data to appear on a product detail page and enables the book to be found in all relevant searches. Some of this can happen overnight from when the data is received, while some occurs during twice-weekly (but sometimes delayed) catalog rebuilds.

These steps, of course, depend on proper processing at Lightning and Ingram as well—and that's part of why I previously discussed checking and correcting your listings there. These two sources, both essential, are normally the *only* two you can count on to supply data to Amazon for a Lightning book. Bowker's Books in Print, for example, may be used by other booksellers, but *not* by Amazon.

Your listing will become functional in dribs and drabs as steps are completed. For instance, a basic listing with Lightning data may show up on Amazon within two days after you approve your Lightning proof—but you may not yet be able to find it by searching on title or author. Instead, search by keyword for your book's ASIN—Amazon Standard Identification Number, identical to the old, 10-digit ISBN—or just swap your ASIN into the following Web address, currently set up for *POD for Profit*.

www.amazon.com/dp/0938497462

The book's availability status too will change as steps are completed. You may first see the book listed as unavailable—but that should change quickly. You may next see availability of 10 to 14 days or longer, which is the time Amazon estimates for receiving copies ordered directly from Lightning. But once the Ingram data arrives, the availability should change quickly to "in stock" and orderable with "one-day shipping," reflecting Amazon's use of Ingram for drop shipping. This is also Amazon's cue that a discount is in order, and you should see that discount within another week or so—at least if the book has begun selling.

How long does the basic listing process take? That depends on the alignment of the stars, plus barometric pressure. Well, actually, it depends partly on the day of the week you approve your Lightning proof, the cooperation of computers, and other factors. But the main variable is how quickly Ingram processes and posts your book data. Normally, you'll see a Lightning book's listing fully functional on Amazon.com in about a week or less. But Ingram takes longer to set up your *first* Lightning book, so the process typically drags on for two to four weeks.

A quick way to check the status of your listing is with my own free online tool Sales Rank Express. S.R.E. results show all essential elements of a book's listing, including availability and discount, while prominently noting any missing elements.

www.salesrankexpress.com

As soon as your listing appears, you can start correcting and adding to it. Basic data corrections are made through Amazon's Catalog Update Form. One way to reach this is through the "update product info" link in the light blue Feedback box near the bottom of your book's detail page. Another is with the "Fix Data" button at Sales Rank Express. You'll need an Amazon customer account to use the form, though you do not need to have made a purchase.

Other info, like your book description, can be added or replaced with Amazon's Books Content Update Form. Find it at

www.amazon.com/add-content-books

It's also linked from the main page of Sales Rank Express.

Though I've pointed out various ways a cover image can get to Amazon, the simplest, most reliable way to replace one is through Amazon Advantage. To access the cover upload feature, you'll need to sign up for a paid account. But you do *not* need to enroll any book (even if you're told that you do)—and of course, when you're working with Lightning, you shouldn't!

advantage.amazon.com

Amazon limits direct contact of its various departments, but you can often get appropriate help through the General Questions contact form. Just use the "Contact Us" button you find on any Amazon Help page, or the link from Sales Rank Express. S.R.E. also offers a link to Amazon's Features and Services contact form.

You might also get assistance from the very helpful staff at Amazon's Author Central, once you've signed up there.

authorcentral.amazon.com

Once Ingram starts sending out info on your book, you may notice it's suddenly available not only from Amazon itself but also from a large number of third-party vendors in Amazon Marketplace—often at prices lower than Amazon's. In fact, the number of Marketplace businesses selling your book may be greater than the number of copies Lightning reports as sold!

Neither these vendors nor Lightning are ripping you off. These vendors don't really have your book at all. If a customer orders it from one of them, they in turn order it from Ingram—just as Amazon might—and you get your payment. What's more, a sale by a third-party vendor is still counted toward your book's Amazon sales rank.

Other copies offered on Marketplace might be review copies you've sent out yourself. Again, no one is ripping you off. Reviewers are free to do whatever they want with books they receive, including sell them on Amazon. If this doesn't suit you, your only recourse is to send out fewer review copies.*

Some Marketplace vendors, though, cause real problems. Some of these rogue sellers will purposely create a duplicate listing of your book to draw away customers and fool them into

---

* For a reviewer who wants to avoid hurting a publisher's sales, the question of what to do with a review copy they don't want to keep is a knotty one. Bringing it to almost any used book store can wind up with the book on Marketplace. On the other hand, few reviewers would feel right about just throwing the book away. My own solution is to donate it to my local library's book sale.

buying it at an inflated price. This violates Amazon policies and should be reported. Check for such vendors with occasional searches on your author name or title keywords, keeping in mind that a duplicate listing might have misspellings and omissions.

Even worse is a vendor who gets hold of Lightning data, legitimately or not, and lists your book on Amazon before Amazon itself has a chance to do so. The signs of such a listing are that it appears just one day after your proof approval, it includes careless errors and omissions, and it shows the book at first being offered not by Amazon but by a single Marketplace vendor. You should complain about this vendor to Lightning—but then you'll also need to correct the listing through Amazon.

In special cases, a Lightning book's listing may have full info, and even show availability from Marketplace vendors, but get stuck short of being shown as available from Amazon itself. You can contact Amazon to point out that your book can now be obtained from Lightning Source and Ingram. Or if Amazon shows a status of "Not Yet Published," you can try the Universal Antidote: Order a copy of your own book. That prompts Amazon to figure out where to get it.

Still another possibility is to ask your Client Services Rep at Lightning to notify its Distribution Issues Team. But since the problem is probably at Amazon, Lightning's chances of solving it are likely no better than your own.

Normally, the data from Lightning will be the first glimpse of your book by Amazon, and that will establish Lightning as the book's *vendor of record*. That means Amazon recognizes Lightning as the primary source for ordering your book and as the prime authority for the book's listing. Changes in data at Lightning should then always be accepted at Amazon—unless Amazon has manually changed the data at your request.

Complications can arise, though, if you've moved a book to Lightning from Amazon Advantage or from Amazon's CreateSpace. If you owned the original ISBN and are still using it after the move, then no new listing is generated—Amazon handles the book through the listing it already has. But in this case the vendor of record has already been established, and any changes you've made in data when setting up the book at Lightning—as well as any changes you make there later—will probably be ignored.

Some of these changes can be made on Amazon with the kinds of corrections and additions we've discussed. But some—like a pricing change—cannot. So, you need to correct the underlying situation. Do that by contacting Amazon and asking it to change the vendor of record from the previous one to Lightning Source. It's better, though, if you made your book at Lightning a new edition with a new ISBN, because you then avoid this issue entirely. (For more on this, see the special section "Moving to Lightning" at the end of this chapter.)

What about prelisting your book for advance sales? Self publishers often ask about that—but I don't recommend it, as it is almost always more trouble than it's worth. (If you'd like to know more about why, see "Prelisting on Amazon" following this section.)

Lightning books are found on Amazon sites also in Canada, the U.K., France, Germany, and Japan. Find them at these addresses.

www.amazon.ca (Canada)
www.amazon.co.uk (U.K.)
www.amazon.fr (France)
www.amazon.de (Germany)
www.amazon.co.jp (Japan)

For listings, those sites get their book info and content from a variety of sources—but not much from each other! Amazon in the U.K. relies for basic info mostly on Nielsen BookData and also receives info direct from Lightning UK. For availability of books not in stock, though, Amazon will check Bertrams|THE and possibly Gardners for copies on hand (instead of just a listing of "Print on Demand"). But since those wholesalers don't drop ship for Amazon in the U.K. as Ingram does in the U.S., you don't get one-day shipping in the U.K. unless Amazon stocks the book.

Amazon in France, Germany, and Japan also gets its info for books in English primarily from Nielsen BookData, possibly supplemented by basic info passed on by Amazon.com. For France and Germany, Amazon might get drop shipping from Gardners for the rare Lightning book that Gardners keeps on hand. But for stocking, Amazon in these three countries might order the book from either the U.K. or the U.S., depending on where it can get the best deal—and nowadays, with the weak dollar and lower printing costs, that's most often the U.S.

As for Amazon in Canada, it can go toward either the U.S. or the U.K. for both info and buying. But it gives priority to the U.S. and to Ingram.

Of course, the need to import books from the U.S. or the U.K. can greatly add to posted availability times. It generally also means a higher price charged by Amazon, through either a reduced discount or a surcharge—though this might be masked by the currency conversion.

The time to appearance of fully functional listings on these sites might be one or two weeks after proof approval at Lightning. Because of the indirect supply chains, though, availability is less predictable.

Overall, the easiest way to check your book listings on Amazon's many sites is through Sales Rank Express. Just click on the tab for the country you want. (If your book is in English but the Amazon site isn't, be sure to select "Imported" in S.R.E.'s search options.) In the results, S.R.E. will even translate many terms into English for you.

Of course, you can also use the sites' own search forms. On the non-English sites, you can find books in English when searching in all departments at once (the default) or when searching just in "English books." You will *not* find them when searching in books in general, or in books in that country's language. Note that your book's ISBN is the same anywhere in the world, so you can search for that on any site, in either its thirteen-digit or its ten-digit form.

As with errors on Amazon.com, errors on these sites are likely to originate upstream, so check there first. If you want to make a change just on the Amazon site, you can reach that site's equivalent of the Catalog Update Form with the link near the bottom of your book's detail page, or with the "Fix Data" button in S.R.E. results.

On these sites too, you'll need a customer account to correct data—but any account you have on Amazon in the U.S., Canada, the U.K., France, or Germany, will carry over to all the rest. So, just sign in with your usual email address and password. At this writing, though, Amazon in Japan makes you create a separate account just for that site. (But you can sign up with the same email address and password as for the others.)

Just as with basic book data, content you submit for your book's detail page is generally not shared among Amazon sites, so you'll have to submit to them individually. All except France have an equivalent of the Books Catalog Update Form. To find the forms, use the links at Sales Rank Express—just click the country tab to view the one you want. Note that, for each site not in English, there's a separate form for English-language books—though the forms themselves aren't in that language.

The main exception to the lack of Amazon sharing is cover images, which migrate almost instantly from one site to all others. If you've gotten your image onto Amazon.com or any of the others, you're all set.

Each site has contact forms reached through its Help pages, including special forms on non-English-language sites for English speakers. You can also reach all of these through links at Sales Rank Express.

Though you may not be able to read forms in languages other than your own, the forms are similar enough to each other that you can often figure out what to put where. One good trick is to view a form in your own language in one browser window, and the same form in a foreign language in another window.

POD books are spread among the Amazon sites also by Marketplace sellers from the U.S. and the U.K. who order from wholesalers and ship internationally. Because of differences in currency and suppliers, this sometimes means Marketplace sellers can substantially undercut Amazon's prices, as U.S. sellers often do on Amazon in the U.K. This also means that a book printed by Lightning will show up on all these sites even if you try to limit distribution.

As in the U.S., if any of these sites have trouble knowing where to get your book, you can tell them—or if the book shows as available at all, just order a copy. (Since overseas shipping can exceed the cost of the book, you might make it a gift to someone in that country.)

For much, *much* more about marketing on Amazon, see my book *Aiming at Amazon*.

Prelisting on Amazon

Self publishers are often eager to *prelist* their book on Amazon—get it listed there before it's actually available—so the book can get preorders. For Amazon sites *outside* the U.S., this is fairly easy to do by listing early at Nielsen BookData. But for Amazon.com—the U.S. site—it's a different story. As I've said, prelisting there is not possible through Lightning Source, because Lightning sends out book data as soon as you approve your proof, and Amazon starts selling as soon as it gets the data.

Prelisting on Amazon.com is possible in other ways, but not without some chicanery and/or complication. For instance, some publishers have set up a book initially with Amazon Advantage, then canceled the book there before having to fill orders. But that causes Amazon to fail to recognize Lightning as the vendor of record, which can give you trouble if you try to change a price.

Similar problems have been caused by attempts to prelist via ipage—which is possible for older Lightning clients with an ipage *publisher* account. These attempts have created a vendor of record problem with Ingram, in which the wholesaler didn't realize it could get the book from Lightning and so failed to even list it as available.

Another problem with prelisting may come if your announced publication date arrives but the book has been delayed. If Amazon thinks the book should be available but knows of no source, it may slap on a "sourcing fee" of several dollars. Then if it decides it simply can't get your book, it will cancel all preorders, inconveniencing and confusing its customers.

The truth is, prelisting on Amazon.com—or on any other Amazon site, for that matter—is seldom worth the bother. Amazon customers are generally reluctant to mess with unknown books that aren't even available yet, so you're not likely to get enough preorders to matter. I suggest you forget prelisting entirely.

Check Other Booksellers

Frankly, I seldom pay much attention to online booksellers other than Amazon. Few can contribute enough sales to warrant it, even if you might personally like them or want to support them. (OK, I'm thinking IndieBound, Powells.com.)

Then there are bookstores that have significant market share but won't let you correct or add to listings. Borders.com, for instance, gets its info from Baker & Taylor and provides no way for a Lightning Source publisher to directly add content—and in any case, Lightning books with short discounts are blocked from the site. Similarly, the online store of Waterstone's in the U.K. draws book info exclusively from Nielsen BookData.

The biggest exception to all this is BarnesandNoble.com—BN.com to its friends. Though its sales may be only 10% of Amazon's, that can still be significant for your book. And any publisher can correct or enhance the book listings there, which as a bonus can also be viewed by customers on terminals in physical Barnes & Noble stores. Find it at

www.bn.com

BN.com can pull book info and cover images directly from Lightning as well as from Ingram, and you should see your book there within a couple of days of approving your proof. In fact, you may see it there even before approval, because BN.com also draws from Bowker's Books in Print, including any publication date you listed there.

Locate BN.com's information for publishers just by clicking on any "Help" link and scrolling down to the relevant section. Be sure to ignore the advice for becoming a "vendor of record." This is for publishers who want to sell directly to

Barnes & Noble—which would mean filling orders yourself and letting B&N dictate discount and terms.

Unlike Amazon, BN.com hasn't set up online forms for data correction and submissions. To correct data, send email to

Corrections@barnesandnoble.com

To add content or cover images, send email to

Titles@bn.com

In either case, be sure to include both title and ISBN for identification.

Be aware, though, that not everything you send may be used. BN.com is geared more toward automated handling of standardized data from regular vendors and can be very careless about manual submissions.

Like Amazon, BN.com can order either from Ingram or direct from Lightning. Also like Amazon, BN.com will have Ingram drop ship a Lightning book not in its own stock. So, books active at Lightning are always listed with 24-hour availability.

If your book starts selling much on BN.com, it will have the book stocked in at least one of the B&N warehouses. This can help B&N store customers get your book more quickly, even if it's not on store shelves. How do you tell if your book is in stock or just being drop shipped? Look on the book's detail page for the "Pick Me Up" search box for locating the book in individual stores. If the search box is there, then the book is in at least one store or warehouse.

If you're outside the U.S., there may be other online booksellers that you'd like to target in your country, if they're open to input. In Canada, for instance, there's chapters.indigo.ca, the online store of Indigo Books & Music. Find it at

www.chapters.indigo.ca

This bookseller is probably Canada's biggest seller of Lightning books next to Amazon.ca—but it is not a Lightning partner and so cannot order the books directly. Instead, it seems to depend for info and ordering on Ingram International, Ingram's exporting division.*

Lightning books may not be listed promptly by Indigo, and they're listed only selectively. Nonfiction and children's books seem to stand a better chance than fiction—but not all nonfiction is accepted either. New Age books, for example, seem less welcome than business books.

Publisher info for this bookseller is at

www.chapters.indigo.ca/vendors

The email address for corrections and additions is

ElectronicData@indigo.ca

To get a quick look at your book at many online booksellers in North America and Europe, you can go to one of the following price comparison sites.

www.booksprice.com
www.bookfinder4u.com
www.fetchbook.info

For an accurate picture, be sure to look at prices without shipping.

---

* Lightning books exported by Ingram International are part of your U.S. sales. They do *not* go through Lightning's Canadian distribution channel and are not transacted in Canadian dollars. At this writing, Lightning's Canadian distribution channel is inactive, except through the Espresso Book Machine.

Moving to Lightning

Are you moving books to Lightning Source from a self publishing company or from Amazon Advantage? Here's the procedure I recommend, aimed to give you the least possible trouble.

1. Submit your book to Lightning as a new edition with a new ISBN.

2. Wait for your new edition on Amazon to show "in stock." This should take about three weeks for your first Lightning book, and about a week for later ones.

3. Wait also for Amazon to copy the old edition's Editorial Reviews, Customer Reviews, tags, and so on to the new edition. If this doesn't happen automatically, contact Amazon to say the two editions should be linked.

4. Stop sales of the old edition. For CreateSpace, for instance, this is done from the Member Dashboard. Go to your book's Title Setup tab, choose "Sales Channel Management," and click on the "Disable" button for Amazon.com. For Amazon Advantage, "Suspend" the book at the "Update Item Status" page on the Items tab.

Note that, with Advantage, you should *not* completely close either the listing or your account. As long as the book is listed, you can use Advantage's Update Item Content form to edit book info for both editions together—and this works better than the Books Content Update Form you'd otherwise have to use. Also, your Advantage account will let you upload cover images for any book at all.

The procedure I gave you assumes that the edition you send Lightning is basically the same as the old. If it's instead a major update or revision, you might want less of an overlap in sales. If so, stop sales of the old edition as soon as you approve your Lightning proof. Or to be more aggressive about it, stop sales at least a month *before* you expect to approve your proof, giving Amazon enough time to sell out its stock. But then you run the risk of too long a gap if you're late with your Lightning edition.

After publishing a new edition through Lightning, self publishers sometimes want Amazon to entirely delist the old one. But because Amazon can still sell used copies—as well as new copies already printed and in the pipeline—it will not do this, and really shouldn't be asked to. Sorry!

If you enjoy living dangerously, you *may* be able to move your book entirely to Lightning in the existing edition with the original ISBN. But for that, two things must be true:

• You obtained the original ISBN yourself instead of getting it from a self publishing company.

• You did *not* publish the book with a self publishing company that used Lightning to print and distribute it. (Most such companies *do* use Lightning for most books.)

Actually, there are only a couple of likely cases that fit these conditions. One is if you printed your book conventionally and sold it through Amazon Advantage. Another is if you published through CreateSpace or BookSurge with your own ISBN and *without* signing up for CreateSpace's Expanded Distribution Channel.

Using the same ISBN in such cases, though, you still run the risk of a "vendor of record" problem, where Amazon won't accept certain book data changes from Lightning or Ingram, including price changes. To take care of that, you want to blot out your book's earlier association as completely as you can.

CreateSpace offers no way to cancel a title completely, but Advantage lets you "Close" the book's listing. This is done through the online contact form. For Issue, choose "Item

Management," and for Subissue, choose "Item Out of Stock/Close Item." Again, do *not* close your entire account.

Next—whether moving from Advantage or CreateSpace—write to Amazon through the General Questions contact form that's accessible from any Help page. Ask for Amazon to note Lightning Source as the new vendor of record for your book, and ask that this request be forwarded to the Books Catalog Department. Hopefully, that will do it—but results are not guaranteed!

By the way, if you close the book's listing in Advantage, you'll receive a very scary email telling you that Amazon may no longer be able to obtain your book. Ignore this, or else print it out and treat it in an appropriately nasty manner. (You have my permission.)

Some self publishers who try Lightning have the idea—at least at first—that they'll keep their bookselling arrangements with CreateSpace or Advantage. There is seldom a good enough reason to do this. The most it is likely to get you is increased labor and/or decreased profit. In fact, a primary reason to use Lightning is that it lets you get around Create-Space and Advantage.

So, don't keep one foot in each camp. Move on boldly, and shake the dust from your feet.

8
Spreading the Word

Show Up Online

If you're at all Web savvy, you should post at least one on-line page of info about your book. This can be on a Web site or a blog or a social networking site, but it should include in one place everything you want potential readers to know. Having such a page is important because it's the *only* place your book will appear where you completely control the content and presentation. Of course, you also want to be able to revise and add to it as needed.

Among the elements that this page might include are
- The full, authoritative title and subtitle.
- A representative graphic.
- Your author name.
- A detailed description.
- Author info.
- Miscellaneous info—format, price, publisher or imprint name, copyright year, page count, trim size, special elements (illustrations, index, glossary), ISBN, LCCN, age level (for kids' books).
- A cover image—maybe even the real one!
- Testimonials, reviews, awards.
- Table of contents.
- Sample text.
- Affiliate links to Amazon.

As examples of one way to fit these together, here are my pages for *Aiming at Amazon* and one other book, which is on a site I maintain as a children's author.

www.newselfpublishing.com/books/
AimingAmazon.html
www.aaronshep.com/books/MouseDeer.html

A Web site of your own requires more work and more skill than a blog or a social networking page—but at the same time, it lets you add more types of material and organize them however you want. Beyond a basic page of book info, possible materials on your Web site include

- Longer excerpts from the book.
- A gallery of photos or other graphics.
- Extended author info.
- A bibliography (with links to Amazon) on the book's subject or a related one.
- A list of relevant links.
- A Web tool, such as a calculator.
- A game.
- Podcasts or other audio recordings.
- A book video.
- A blog!

The point of all this is to be useful and/or interesting, not just to deliver a sales pitch. That's what will draw people to your site, inspire them to link to you, get you mentioned in their blogs, and so on.

But before any of that can happen, they must first be able to find you, and that means providing full access and complete information to search engines so they can properly index your site. Unfortunately, this is where many sites fail, because many consumer Web design programs, as well as many professional Web designers, focus more on appearance than function.

To design your site for good exposure in search engines, you may need to delve into the more obscure features of your program, or even into the underlying HTML source code. Or if the work is being done for you, you may have to be explicit about what you expect.

An important part of what search engines look for is in the Web page's HTML *head*—a section of code that is not displayed on the page but that provides document info plus instructions to browsers. Your Web design program might let you view and edit this code, or else you can open your file in a text editor like Notepad (Windows) or TextEdit (Mac). Do not open the file in a word processor—or at least don't save it from one—or you'll probably ruin it!

Here's a stripped-down version of what you might see near the top.

```
<html>
<head>
<title>Untitled</title>
<meta http-equiv="content-language" content="en">
<meta http-equiv="content-type" content=
        "text/html; charset=utf-8">
<meta name="description" content="">
<meta name="keywords" content="">
</head>
```

The most important line here for you is the one with the two "title" tags. (The first is an opening tag, and the one with the slash is a closing tag.) Between the tags is your page's HTML title. If you have not supplied your own text for this, you'll probably see something generic, like the name of the file or of the entire site.

Though this text is not displayed on your Web page proper, it does appear along the top edge of your visitor's browser window or on their browser tab. But that's not the main reason it's important. It's important because Google and other search engines use it as your page's title in search results and also give it high priority in figuring out what your page is about.

The HTML title, then, while providing a concise description of the page's subject and positioning within your Web site, should also include all the most important related keywords. Here it is for the *Aiming at Amazon* info page.

> <title>Books ~ Aiming at Amazon (Self Publishing, Print on Demand, Online Book Marketing, Amazon.com)</title>

The "description" meta tag is important as well. This too is used by the search engines to figure out your content, and it may also be quoted directly in search results. Here's what it looks like for my *Aiming at Amazon* page.

> <meta name="description" content="Book info for 'Aiming at Amazon: The NEW Business of Self Publishing, or How to Publish Your Books with Print on Demand and Online Book Marketing on Amazon.com.'">

Finally, the "keywords" meta tag should include *all* keywords related to the page, with the most important ones first. Search engines don't give as much weight to this tag as they used to, but supplying keywords here is still worth the effort. In fact, if you include words or variants not found in your text, it may be the only reason your book shows up for a particular search at all. Here's how it looks for my *Aiming at Amazon* page.

> <meta name="keywords" content="Lightning Source Inc., LSI, print on demand, printing on demand, publishing on demand, books on demand, POD publisher, POD publishers, self publishing company, self publishing companies, Amazon, Amazon.com, selfpublishing, online book marketing, publicity, desktop publishing, autopublicación, autoédition,

autopublication, auto-édition, individu-édition, publication, publicación, Selbstverlag, Selbst Verlag, 自費出版, book, books">

Within the actual content of the page, some of the elements most important to search engines are the headings—the displayed page title and subheadings. In the HTML code, you should see this text surrounded by the heading tags <h1> . . . </h1>, <h2> . . . </h2>, <h3> . . . </h3>, and so on, with the lower numbers showing higher levels. Headings are given significant weight by the search engines—in fact, the top heading is probably second in importance only to the HTML title. For best results, make sure these headings feature your most important keywords.

As for the rest of the page, you'll want to liberally sprinkle it with keywords, stopping well short of being obnoxious. Make sure you use the full form of names as often as you can without being awkward. For instance, if you were writing about Lightning Source, you would say "Lightning Source" frequently, not only "Lightning" or "LSI."

Also helpful are links to relevant, authoritative pages. These can be links from terms or names within the text, or links in lists of additional resources.

Besides the things you should do for search engines, there are things you should *not*. For example, many Web sites you see nowadays have headings in fancy fonts or formatting. Most pro Web designers favor such designs, and many Web design programs employ this approach. Though such headings certainly look nice, their text must be rendered as graphics, and *search engines can't read it.* You therefore lose much of your chance at getting good search results placement. If you can't stop your program or your designer from converting headings to graphics, you need a new program or designer!

Other no-no's include structuring your Web site with HTML frames—search engines can't access the content—and creating links with JavaScript—search engines can't follow those links. The simpler your site, the better the search engines will like it.

You may find and benefit from other ways to optimize your pages for search engines, but do *not* get caught up in tricky, deceptive schemes. If they work at all, it's usually only for the short time it takes for the search engines to catch on— and at that point, you may even be penalized. Meanwhile, you may well have alienated your visitors too.

Always remember, the key to getting Web traffic is to provide compelling content. Yes, make sure your site is respectably presented and reasonably friendly to search engines. But then stop worrying about all that and focus on giving your visitors what they came for.

Your Web site may be aimed not only at visitors you hope will buy your book, but also at those who already have. For example, your site might include

- Updates to the book.
- Content that didn't quite fit.
- Enhanced graphics—for instance, photos in color instead of black and white.
- And of course, info on any other books of yours.

To draw existing readers to your Web site, be sure your book prominently displays your Web address! For example, you might place it once on the back cover and repeat it one or more times inside, like so.

www.newselfpublishing.com

(Sorry, couldn't resist.)

Your Web site should also include ways for you to communicate with your visitors. You should *never* post your email address on your site, because it will invite spam. But a properly-designed contact form should allow messages to be sent to you without revealing your address.

For talking to your readers and visitors, you might set up an email bulletin. This can be done as a one-way list through Yahoo Groups or Google Groups, with sign-up forms placed prominently around your site. Such a bulletin doesn't have to take much of your time if you use it just for occasional notices and announcements. And you'll be glad you have it when you get around to publishing your next book.

Web sites can consume enormous amounts of time and mental energy if you let them. So, it's fair to ask: Do I really need to deal with all this? The answer is no. What you do on Amazon alone can be enough to generate satisfying sales there with no recourse to a Web site at all.

In fact, depending on your subject, a Web site may not generate many sales of your book at all, even if the site is popular. My publishing buddy Morris Rosenthal, who has focused on books about computers and publishing, swears by his site and considers it his top tool for generating sales. My own children's author site, likewise very popular but aimed mostly at teachers and librarians, has proven far less effective in that. My view is that people who want to buy books mostly go to Amazon, while people who want freebies surf the Web.

Still, some Web sites do generate sizeable sales. And even a few sales directed to Amazon can make a significant difference to your book, especially in its early days. So, if you have the time and energy—or if you're eager, as I am, to share your content worldwide, even apart from your books or any financial payback—then building up your Web site may well be worthwhile.

Get Reviews

Once you have some printed books in hand, you might want to send them to any good-sized magazines, newsletters, or other periodicals geared toward your subject matter or genre. Since nearly all now have a Web presence, they shouldn't be hard to search out. Reviews from such periodicals may not sell many books directly, but comments taken from them can certainly make your book look good on your online book info page and elsewhere.

Small publishers in the U.S. are usually told to submit their books to the major review journals geared toward libraries and the book trade. These are *Publishers Weekly,* the American Library Association's *Booklist, Kirkus Reviews,* and either *Library Journal* (for adult books) or *School Library Journal* (for children's books).

A good review in one of these can certainly be lucrative, but there are reasons you should think twice about pursuing this. First off, *Publishers Weekly* would want your book to be aimed at bookstores, with conventional design and standard terms—so if you're following my publishing plan, you're already out. *Kirkus* has a flat policy against reviewing self-published books. The rest have no such rule but seldom review them anyway—and when they do, their reviews can be much less lenient than those of the average Amazon customer.

The main problem, though, is that reviews from most of these journals are licensed by Amazon.com and included with your book's "Editorial Reviews." And they're displayed *first.* Since Amazon allows only two elements from this group to appear on your book's detail page, two reviews from major journals would push all your own submitted material off that page. That might be fine if the reviews are glowing, but if one or both are bad? You have a disaster.

Here's my recommendation: If you're feeling lucky enough to bother with any such journals, forget all of them except *Booklist*. Unlike the others, *Booklist* has a policy of reviewing only books it recommends—so you don't have to worry about Amazon permanently displaying a bad review. Also, with only one such submission, you run no risk of your material getting pushed off your book's detail page. And your chances of getting reviewed are best with *Booklist* anyway, because it reviews by far the most books.

Submission requirements are at

www.booklistonline.com

Like the other major review journals, *Booklist* encourages you to submit about four months before your pub date, and in the prepublication format of a *galley* or *advance reading copy* (ARC).* But this is not a strict requirement, and the off-chance of getting reviewed isn't worth the hassle of producing an additional format, or the possible sales loss from delaying publication. So my advice is, just send copies of the finished book, whenever it's available.

Be sure to send a copy also to Jim Cox's *Midwest Book Review,* which aims to support small publishers. It issues dependably positive reviews and posts them in a number of places online, including on Amazon as customer reviews under the *Review's* name. Find info at

www.midwestbookreview.com

---

* That's "advance," not "advanced."

The *Review* accepts no money from publishers, but donations of stamps are welcomed!

For each review copy you send out, attach a slip or self-adhesive labels inside the front cover with all basic info about the book. Here's what I included for *Aiming at Amazon*.

TITLE: Aiming at Amazon
SUBTITLE: The NEW Business of Self Publishing
AUTHOR: Aaron Shepard
PUBLISHER: Shepard Publications
US DISTRIBUTION: Ingram, Baker & Taylor
UK DISTRIBUTION: Gardners, Bertrams
ISBN: 978-0-938497-43-1
LC: 2006907458
CIP: No
SIZE: 6 x 9
PAGES: 174
FORMAT: Paperback
BACK MATTER: Index
WEB MATTER: Resource lists, updates
PRICE: $16.00

PUBLICATION DATE: Jan. 1, 2007

CONTACT PHONE: 555-555-5555
EMAIL: Shepard2007@shepardpub.com
WEB: www.shepardpub.com

PLEASE SEND REVIEW TO:
Shepard Publications
555 Olympia Ave NE, #55
Olympia, WA 98506

Note that the distributor is technically Lightning Source, but I cited wholesalers instead to avoid a blatant flag of self publishing. Also note the minimized subtitle.

Another, newer way to get reviews is to target bloggers, if there are any writing about your field or genre. These people are often eager to find content for their pages, so they're likely to welcome a review copy of your book. An added benefit of their attention is that you get links leading to your book info on Amazon or on your own site. You might also get an online conversation rolling that extends to bloggers beyond the ones you contacted.

Because of the high number of potential reviewers among bloggers and others on the Web—and because some of their audiences may be tiny—you might choose to serve some or all of them with electronic copies instead of printed ones. As long as you work out clear policies and stick to them, no one should be offended. In fact, some reviewers may *prefer* electronic copies, because they'll arrive quickly.

As a self publisher, you're likely to come across services offering to provide book reviews for pay. I've never used such a service, and I hope I'd never get that desperate. In the eyes of the general consumer, a good testimonial can be as effective as a good review, while a book trade professional will likely spot a paid review as such. Though some such paid services are surely well-meaning, there are also far too many people eager to make money off novice self publishers on services of little or no value.

While working out your strategy for review copies, don't neglect the review copy's poor relation, the news release—formerly called "press release." A *brief* news release about your book should accompany every print or electronic review copy you send out—but it can also be sent out alone when sending a review copy wouldn't be appropriate or worthwhile. For many media outlets, a news release actually works better, because they don't have time or space to review the book. You may find them passing along much or all of your release verbatim.

Note that I am *not* recommending you pay a service to distribute your news release. These services send out such a flood of releases that media professionals have mostly learned to ignore them. And though such a service may generate some links to your Web site, many of those links will come from spam sites that won't help you.

Much more can be said about book reviews and news releases—but it already has been, so I won't try to repeat it here. Find it on the Web or in any general book on self publishing or book marketing. Also, *Aiming at Amazon* offers tips on obtaining testimonials—which can be just as effective as reviews or more so.

Taking It Easy

No matter how extensively I describe my marketing techniques, I still get questions from readers that boil down to, "What *else* should I do?"

The answer may well be, "Nothing."

There are two different ways in which many new self publishers tend to overspend: with their time and with their money. The first can leave you spinning your wheels, while the second can load your book with a burden it may never overcome.

The urge to overspend money most often comes from the drive to create a bestseller. Almost every writer believes their book can be one. That's just part of the territory, and though nearly always completely unrealistic, it's nothing to be ashamed of. I've done it often enough myself! The problem comes when you, as self publisher, let that belief jeopardize your chance of financial success.

One of the beauties of print on demand is that it enables you to publish a book for a relatively small initial outlay. But that won't do you a lick of good if you spoil it by spending thousands and thousands of dollars on marketing.

Let's take the case of Big Trader Guy. Big Trader Guy was a prodigy who had made an enormous amount of money in the stock market at an amazingly young age and then lost much of it. He had written up his story, and armed with his copy of *Aiming at Amazon,* he was ready to unleash his guaranteed bestseller on the world. He was even set to write a sequel on how he made millions of dollars as a self publisher!

But he made two mistakes. The first was to think he could produce a huge bestseller through POD self publishing. Though this isn't strictly impossible, bestsellers nearly always require not only heavy-duty marketing but also heavy-duty distribution. He didn't have the infrastructure. My book had shown him how to get the highest profit per copy, but on top of that, he wanted and expected what my plan could *not* provide: the highest volume of sales. For that, he needed a traditional publisher—and sad to say, he had already turned one away.

His second mistake was to spend over $50,000 to launch the book. Yes, you read that figure right. Though a small portion of that was editorial and production costs, more of it was hiring a publicist and funding a marketing campaign. For instance, a full $6,000 went toward a three-minute author video for the book's page on Amazon.

The book had a lot going for it: an entertaining story, a popular topic, an author with energy, charisma, and ongoing TV exposure, and of course, the tips found in my book. Because of all of that plus his promotional efforts, the book was an immediate success, at one point landing in Amazon's top 1,000 and going on to sell 4,000 copies in four months. But the sales generated by his marketing campaign still had to pay off that campaign's cost—so in the end, he probably lost in expenses as much as the campaign gained him in direct income.

Still, Big Trader Guy was lucky. His book was strong enough to eventually recover from the outlay—and he wound up making high profits on associated products. But for most self publishers who try the bestseller route, the result is simply disastrous loss, financially condemning books that would otherwise have done just fine.

Unlike most schemes to create bestsellers, the promotional techniques I recommend cost nothing or next to nothing. They'll never burden you with overhead you must struggle to pay off before your book can succeed. You can feel more confident about recovering your costs, and with even a modestly successful book, you can start enjoying your profits within months, or even weeks.

But maybe you're not tempted to spend too much money—or maybe you have no money to be tempted with. Your time, though, may be another matter.

So, it's important to understand that your most important efforts extend only to the period around your book's launch. If you've done everything well to that point, Amazon's mechanisms should take over and build your book's position. This process is slow—normally taking one full year to realize the book's sales potential—but it's inexorable. Besides monitoring for glitches, there's not a lot you can do on Amazon to alter it. (At least, not honestly or ethically, which is the only way I recommend.)

One of the biggest competitors to *Aiming at Amazon* is a book that details things you can do on Amazon.com to draw attention to your own book. It focuses on such methods as creating Listmania lists, social networking on Amazon, and posting positive customer reviews for other books while mentioning your own. This book's customer reviews praise the book highly for revealing the secrets of success on Amazon.

I've tried to understand the excitement this book generates. (That is, the genuine part. Most of its customer reviews are obviously written by self publishers promoting their own books in following this one's advice.) After all, much of it is inaccurate, and much of the rest is now outdated. And most of the methods it recommends most highly—even setting aside their spammy nature, questionable ethics, and occasional violation of Amazon guidelines—simply aren't very effective, as suggested by the author's own lack of prior publishing success.

I've finally had to conclude that the book is popular because it *keeps authors and self publishers busy*. It occupies them with tasks that make them imagine they're accomplishing something. Meanwhile, the *real* work is being done behind the scenes by Amazon—if the book is going anywhere at all.

I guess this is why my competitor's book—which flatly contradicts mine in many ways—is often said to complement it. My book keeps you busy through your book's launch—when it matters most—while that one keeps you busy from then on—when it matters far less.

What about things you can do *off* Amazon to keep building your sales? Sure, there are a ton of them—enough to take up every available minute of your time. You can build a Web site, you can write a blog, you can contribute to Yahoo groups, you can interact with social networks—there's no end to it. I even do some of it myself. But it's all peripheral, because most of the book *buyers* are on Amazon, and Amazon's automatic systems for promoting books are advanced beyond anything you can devise.

Besides, getting people talking about your book doesn't necessarily require doing much talking yourself. If you've produced something that people value, they'll spread the word on their own. In fact, they may talk about it more if you're *not* hanging around to push it.

Truthfully, the best thing you can do for both your book and your publishing business is to create *new* books for Amazon's systems to promote. Each new successful book will boost the others in a multiplier effect.

Or take some time off. Spend the day with your family. Go to the beach. Take a trip. Whether or not you're watching, fretting, tinkering, or spending, Amazon and Lightning Source will be doing their jobs, selling your books, generating your income, day after day after day.

9
Looking at Legalities

Consider Copyright

Now, I know that some of you are waiting with bated breath for me to talk about registering your copyright. So, let me explain something about copyright law.

In the U.S. and most other countries in the world, you own the copyright to your writing, whether or not you place a copyright notice in your book. You own the copyright even if the book is never published. And most especially, you own the copyright without signing forms and paying a fee to any official agency.

In the U.S., official copyright registration provides extra financial benefits if a case involving that copyright ever goes to court. But the copyright is yours whether you register it or not. I'm not going to tell you not to register your U.S. copyright, but unless you have the stomach to bring a copyright infringement case to trial, registration is not likely to do you any good.

In fact, it probably won't do you any good anyway, because the chances of a truly harmful infringement on your book's copyright are extremely slim. Other than in the case of bestsellers, most instances of infringement are penny-ante stuff like photocopying of chapters or file sharing among people who wouldn't buy your book anyway. Not the kind of thing a self publisher should have to lose sleep over—or anyone else, for that matter. By the time you're popular enough to lose much money from illegal copying, you're rich enough that you don't need to care.

Besides, don't you know that theft is often the most cost-efficient method of promotion? This principle is well-known in the software world, where it was a key to the ascendancy of Microsoft Word. That's one reason to take the view of the venerable Ruth Stout: "It's a fair-sized job to write a book that people can be bothered just to read; when they begin to steal copies, you are really getting some place."

I realize that some of you will never feel secure without that copyright certificate in your hand, and some of you may even be among those rare individuals who would actually benefit. So, if you *must* register a U.S. copyright, you can do it at the site of the U.S. Copyright Office, at

www.copyright.gov

Canada too offers optional copyright registration. Get info from the site of the Canadian Intellectual Property Office, at

www.cipo.ic.gc.ca

Most other countries have *no* option for official copyright. But if you're determined to register regardless, there are commercial agencies that will gladly take your money. One that offers that service internationally is Copyright Witness, at

www.copyrightwitness.com

Its U.K. branch, known as The U.K. Copyright Service, is at

www.copyrightservice.co.uk

Make a Deposit

In the U.S., you must send one or two copies of your book to the Library of Congress *if* you register copyright or *if* you received either a Library of Congress Control Number or Cataloging in Publication. (See my earlier discussions of these programs.) Otherwise, there's no such obligation, and you are not even encouraged to do so.

Could you just send one if you really wanted to? Good question!

In most other countries, though, you must *always* send one or more copies of your book to your national library. This is called *legal deposit*. Here are info links for various countries.

> **www.bl.uk/aboutus/stratpolprog/legaldep**
> (U.K.)
> **www.collectionscanada.gc.ca/legal-deposit**
> (Canada)
> **www.nla.gov.au/services/ldeposit.html**
> (Australia)
> **www.natlib.govt.nz/services/get-advice/**
> **publishing/legal-deposit** (New Zealand)

For other countries, search the Web for "legal deposit" (with quote marks around it) and the country name.

Why This Book Has No Checklist

Every publisher and every book requires a different set of tasks and a different schedule for them. There's no way for me to tell you exactly what to do or when to do it.

Part of the process of becoming a publisher is to decide all that for yourself. If you'd rather avoid it, there are many consultants and self publishing companies eager to serve you.

10
Minding Your Business

Watch Your Sales

Though there are a number of ways to monitor how your book is doing, your ultimate source of info will be Lightning Source itself. From Lightning you'll get monthly statements on sales, broken down by title, with both monthly figures and cumulative totals for year to date.

These statements will come separately for each "market," which is defined both by where the book is printed and by the currency of payment. At this writing, that means you'll get one statement from Lightning US for sales in U.S. dollars, and another from Lightning UK for sales in British pounds. The "European" market is not yet active, because Lightning's distribution partners in mainland Europe still buy from the U.K. in pounds. Also inactive is the "Canadian" market, where Lightning has *no* partners yet, and where booksellers are generally supplied from the U.S. by Ingram International, the export arm of Ingram Book Company.

Theoretically, you might get another set of statements for markets in which your book has sold through the Espresso Book Machine. But at this writing, I have yet to hear of a single sale through this channel for any self publisher. (Which is why I don't say much about the Espresso in this book.)

Note that Lightning's statements are for *nominal* months, not actual ones, with the exact period being specified on the statement. That's because they're set up to match Ingram's reporting periods, which include only full weeks ending on Fridays, except at the turn of the year. So, most "months" will have four weeks, while March, June, September, and December will have five to make up the difference. Of course, this irregularity makes it a bit dicey to compare one month's sales figures to another's, unless you first figure weekly averages.

Lightning's statements usually arrive by email in the first week of the month for the month previous. That's *just* the statements, not the payments, which come three months later—a typical delay in the book industry, designed to allow for returns. (Payment—at least by check—is held even longer if the amount you've earned is below a very reasonable minimum.)

If you can't wait so long for the report, or if you want to check mid-month, you can head to Lightning's Web site, where the same information can be requested from the Publisher Compensation form under "My Account." Apart from a freeze of several days at the close of a reporting period, figures are updated each morning that Lightning ships books—Tuesday through Saturday, usually between 7:00 a.m. and 8:00 a.m.*

You can choose dates and other parameters for your report. For dates, choosing an "LSI Period" may work better than setting a "Date Range." (To see a list of reporting period start and end dates, click on the phrase "LSI Period" itself.) Reports can be viewed online or emailed to you.

Note, though, that the figures given online are meant only as estimates. Depending on Lightning's invoicing schedule, the figures on your final statement may vary. If you allow returns, these too can cause differences in your statement, and even later on, in Lightning's payment.

Your statements will reflect seasonal fluctuations—most books sell more in winter than in summer. Even ignoring that, you may see highly irregular sales from month to month. This most likely indicates that one or more booksellers are ordering quantities to keep in stock.

Stock? But isn't print on demand all about *not* keeping books in stock? Well, not exactly. Lightning does not stock its

---

* These hours come from the early-rising and—by his description—obsessive W. F. Zimmerman of Nimble Books.

books, but wholesalers or online retailers might—especially if your book starts to sell well.

Orders for stocking are most likely to come from Amazon, though they might instead come from Ingram or BN.com. At some times of year, Amazon might hold off on such orders, then send all the amassed ones together—so if you have multiple titles, your overall sales swings can be quite large.

Because large stocking orders can either precede or follow heavy consumer sales, keep in mind that the months Lightning sells the most books for you can be different from the months most of them sell to the final customer.

One thing that Lightning's statements will *not* tell you is *who* is buying your book. For that info, you can ask your Client Services Rep for the report "Distribution Sales by Publisher and Channel Customer," which breaks down sales by bookseller for either Lightning US or Lightning UK. For even more detail, you can ask for the report "Orders by Pub ID," which adds dates of ordering, printing, and shipping, and covers all markets together. These reports are compiled for the dates you request, without regard to Lightning's standard reporting periods.

But even with these extra reports, you won't know exactly how many books are ending up where. That's because many of the books will go to wholesalers, and you can't find out who's ordering from those. For example, you might see that Amazon accounts for 65% of your orders from Lightning US—but another 30% might be going to Ingram, and Amazon might be ordering your book from there too. So, what's Amazon's combined total? There's no way to know. (But if you're following my basic publishing plan, it's probably between 75% and 90%.)

Something else you can't know for sure is what *country* your books are going to. Booksellers in the U.S. and Canada generally buy books printed by Lightning US, and booksellers in the U.K. generally buy copies printed by Lightning UK—and that will likely make up the bulk of your sales. But keep in mind that booksellers in any other country might buy from either one, and so might Amazon Marketplace sellers in any country at all.

It's common for new Lightning publishers to hang on their computers trying to correlate Amazon sales—as reflected by jumps in sales rank—to Lightning sales. When they fail to do so, they may conclude that Lightning's reporting is faulty or even dishonest. So, let me state in the strongest terms that italics can convey, *There is no correlation in time between Amazon sales and Lightning sales.* (Please don't make me go to bolding or all caps!)

Yes, all Lightning books sold on Amazon must at some point come from Lightning. But the Lightning sale of any particular copy may be posted days after the Amazon sale—or may already have been posted days, weeks, or even months earlier—and sometimes not even where you'd expect. I've touched on most of this already, but let me summarize the reasons that Amazon sales and Lightning reports might seem not to match up.

First, here are reasons a Lightning sale might not show up till *after* the Amazon sale.

• Amazon sales rank reflects a sale within a couple of hours of ordering, but Lightning records a sale when the printed book is sent out. So, when Amazon orders a Lightning book for drop shipping by Ingram, there is a built-in lag of at least one day. And if the order arrives at Ingram on Saturday, the book won't be printed till Monday or shipped and recorded till Tuesday. In the U.K., Amazon will order direct from Lightning when out of stock, and Lightning may take several days to ship.

- Lightning might be running behind. (A significant delay is rare, but possible.)
- Lightning's reported sales figures freeze for several days at the close of a reporting period. A sale during that time won't appear till updates resume.

Now let's look at cases in which Lightning might report a sale *earlier*.

- Amazon might sell the book from its own stock. At this writing, for popular Lightning books, Amazon tries to keep enough stock on hand to cover about three weeks of sales. This alone can mean an Amazon sale may take place the month *after* Lightning records its own. And if Amazon over-orders, possibly due to a sales spike, a copy may languish in stock for months—well, really, for any amount of time since the book's publication.
- If Amazon orders the book from Ingram, Gardners, or Bertrams, the wholesaler might sell it from stock. Wholesalers don't usually stock Lightning books, but they can if a book is returnable and/or popular. This too can mean a sale by Lightning in a month prior to the final sale.

Finally, here are reasons the sale might not show up at all—or at least, not where you're looking.

- The book was a used or review copy sold in Marketplace. You'd see the same jump in sales rank as for a new book, but there would be no Lightning sale.
- The book was sold in Marketplace by an international vendor. Both U.S. and U.K. vendors can sell on any Amazon site, so the sold copy might not come from the country you expect. This is especially true for the U.K., where current printing prices and exchange rates favor U.S. vendors. So, the sale you may be looking for at Lightning UK may actually have been made by Lightning US.

• The book was sold by Amazon but was ordered from a different country than you expect. Books sold by Amazon in Canada, France, Germany, and Japan come from either Lightning US or Lightning UK, depending on where Amazon's costs come out cheaper. And so far, they do *not* go through Lightning's Canadian or European Union channels—though that may change.

• You double source your book with another POD provider, and the copy sold by Amazon or a Marketplace vendor came from there. For instance, if you double source with TextStream, the copy might have come from Baker & Taylor.

Finally, keep in mind that sales cannot always be determined from sales ranks. If your book's rank jumps from 100,000 to 20,000, then yes, you've made at least one sale. But if it jumps from 20,000 to 19,000, there's no way to know. Because of the way Amazon figures its ranks, your book may rise with no sale at all, only because other books have dropped down.

All this is not to say that Lightning can make no mistake. With computers, anything is possible. So, if you have convincing evidence, by all means, contact Lightning. The address for this is

AccountsPayable@lightningsource.com

But in any case, I can tell you that Lightning's integrity and honesty are not questioned by those who have long worked with it. In the unlikely event you do uncover an error, realize it is just that—an error, not any attempt to cheat or defraud you. Lightning's business depends on the trust of its publisher clients, and it does its very best to earn it.

Sales Trivia

An examination of Lightning Source's "Orders by Pub ID" report, which you can request from your Client Services Rep, can yield some interesting observations. Here, for example, are tidbits I gleaned from the report for Shepard Publications for December 2009.

• Stocking orders from Amazon.com generally fell on Tuesdays, though sometimes with a delay to Wednesday. (It's likely that Amazon ordering is on a weekly cycle of rotation, so that orders for books by other publishers fell on different days.) Orders for individual titles ranged in size from one to fifteen copies, with an average of three. As many as seven of these orders were received for the same title on the same day—suggesting that Amazon may log orders daily, then send them out weekly.

• Barnes & Noble's direct orders to Lightning were all for single copies.

• Baker & Taylor, the wholesaler, collected backorders and ordered from Lightning once a week.

• Lightning's guaranteed overnight fulfillment apparently applies *only* to orders from Ingram. *All* other orders were typically filled in about three business days. Tuesday's Amazon stocking orders, for example, were usually shipped and reported on Friday.

Handle Other Sellers

No single publishing plan is optimum for all situations. You have to set up your terms and procedures to work best for you and your books in the majority of cases. As the Russians say, "Chase two rabbits and catch none."

This may mean sometimes losing orders or even declining to fill them. Now and then, though, you might get an order that doesn't fit your primary plan but that you don't want to turn away either. For those times, you might want to put together an alternate set of terms and procedures.*

For instance, I publish a series of reader's theater script collections, and schools sometimes order classroom sets of a title through a local bookseller. Though the books are normally at short discount, I can hardly expect a bookseller to order so many copies at once from Ingram or Baker & Taylor at no profit. So, as a courtesy, I offer a higher discount on bulk orders through my publisher Web site. This is helpful also when soapmaking suppliers want to stock my wife, Anne's, soapmaking book, as most don't deal with any book wholesaler at all.

At the same time, I certainly don't want to encourage a lot of direct orders—especially at the higher discount—and I also don't want to chase retailers for payment. So, along with a high minimum order and my usual refusal of returns, I require prepayment by PayPal, or at least by check.

---

* At least in the U.S., you can legally offer different terms *only* if the buyer is in a different class, or if the sale falls in a different category. But this is seldom an issue, because *you* define the buyer class and the sales category—for instance, all books under 100 pages sold in quantities of three to shoe repair shops. As long as your policies are well-defined and consistent, you should be within the law. (Not that it's likely anyone would hassle you about it anyway.)

Taken together, these terms are enough to discourage any bookseller who doesn't really need to order direct. You can find more details at

www.shepardpub.com/terms.html

You don't need to keep a stock of books on hand just to fill an occasional large, direct order. Instead, it's convenient and economical to fulfill such orders through Lightning Source. Simply tell Lightning to print and ship the books but to substitute your customer's shipping address for your own. The books will be sent with your return address on the label.

Filling international orders is almost as easy as filling ones at home. You can have books printed and shipped by either Lightning US or Lightning UK, depending on which of your Lightning accounts you're logged into. (If you don't know how to access one or the other, contact your Sales Rep.) When shipping to any country other than those two, don't try to save money by choosing a method without tracking, because international shipments do sometimes get lost.

For those international shipments, you might want to compare total fulfillment costs for Lightning US and Lightning UK. You can do this by accessing each of your Lightning accounts in a different browser, going partway through the ordering process in each, then completing the order that costs least. (Just be sure to delete the order you don't finish, or Lightning will save it for you.) The results could surprise you. International shipping from the U.K. tends to be much cheaper, but so do U.S. printing costs, and a weakened dollar may further alter the equation.

You can ask Lightning to rush your order for a small fee. It will usually be handled within two or three days anyway—but to be safe, you might want to pay the fee during September and December busy seasons.

Do you have a favorite local independent store where you'd like to see your book? If such a store agrees to carry it, they'll most likely say their policy is to buy from local authors on consignment only. That means you'd have to come back regularly and check their stock and then request payment for any copies sold. My advice is to state politely that selling on consignment is against *your* policy, but since they're a local store, you'd be glad to forgo your normal minimum order requirement and shipping fee while giving them a 35% or 40% discount.

Though Lightning supplies all the top wholesalers, there are many other wholesalers it doesn't—mostly small ones catering to libraries. If your book is well received, you may well receive special orders from such wholesalers, requesting a copy or two. It would be nice to support these wholesalers, but for a self publisher aiming at Amazon, it simply isn't worth the hassle.

I suggest you instead reply with a form letter explaining that your book is distributed by Lightning Source and that you do not accept direct orders from wholesalers. For a single copy or two, they'll probably go ahead and order it from Amazon.

These are the policies and procedures I've developed over the years. As an alternative, you might look at CreateSpace Direct, an element in CreateSpace's Expanded Distribution Channel. At this writing, plans are for a Web site to sell Create-Space books at discount to qualified U.S. resellers. You can choose this *without* enabling CreateSpace sales to Amazon, ensuring that Amazon itself keeps buying from Lightning

Though CreateSpace requires a 60% discount for this service, the convenience you gain might be worth it. Note, though, that CreateSpace does not offer all the same trim sizes as Lightning.

Sell Foreign Rights

You might never get an offer to buy foreign rights for one of your books—but then again, you might. In case you do, here are a few tips.

There are basically two kinds of foreign rights you might be asked for: the right to sell your book in English in another country, and the right to sell a translation. I suggest you turn down all English-language rights requests, for two reasons. First, your book either is already selling in that other country or soon will be. Second, that other edition will eventually find its way to your own primary markets, competing with your edition and stealing sales. The book market is increasingly international, and you don't want to share English-language rights with anyone.

As for selling translation rights, if you get an offer from a reputable publisher, there's not much reason to turn it down. But depending on how you arrange it, this can be a fairly simple, pleasant transaction or an ongoing source of frustration. And the difference boils down largely to whether or not you insist on royalties.

The problem is that many publishers are not very good about issuing statements and paying royalties, and the problem seems to grow greater when you're dealing with publishers overseas. Add in language differences, and you can have a maddening mess that recurs each time payment is due.

One solution is to get yourself a foreign rights agent to handle both negotiations and collections. But if your chances of sales are few and far between, this may not be worth the trouble. The other solution is to sell only for a one-time fee, preferably with cash in advance. You can usually get a single payment without too much trouble, and then you can just forget about it.

Rights sales take time and effort while not usually yielding a great deal of money. For that reason, I try to keep things as simple as possible. For one thing, I don't bother with a lot of negotiation. I offer a fair price, based on a one-time payment—often a nice, round thousand dollars. If that's too high for the other publisher, I ask what they can afford. As long as the counter-offer still seems fair, and enough to pay for my own processing, I accept it.

I also try to keep things simple in regard to foreign taxes. Some foreign countries insist on piles of paperwork with supporting evidence and certification to prove they shouldn't claim a deduction from your payment before it's sent to you. Instead of beating my brain over it, I just let the other government take its cut.

Another potential problem is how to deposit payments in foreign currency. In most banks, this is a time-consuming hassle, and some smaller ones can't do it at all without sending your deposit to a third-party service for a hefty fee. You can try to avoid this situation by asking the publisher to pay in U.S. dollars. If that fails, you can ask for payment by PayPal. If that too is unworkable, most large banks have a bank-by-mail service. You can mail a foreign check with a deposit slip and let them convert it on their own time.

Of course, if you start selling foreign rights, you must keep careful records of *exactly* what rights you sell. You don't want to accidentally sell overlapping rights to two publishers. That could get extremely sticky!

11
Facing the Future

Consider Revision

One of the beauties of print on demand is that it's so easy to revise your book. Or at least, that's how it *should* be. When working with Lightning Source, though, the reality is sometimes different.

To make changes, you upload your revised file or files to Lightning and optionally order a proof. Go to "Title Information," click on your book, then on "Upload Revision." Note that, if your revision produced a change in your book's page count, you must inform Lightning on submission. Also, with a new page count, Lightning will insist on a new cover file, whether or not there's any significant difference in spine width.

Within the U.S., your revision can normally be processed within a week—the same amount of time taken for a new book. Lightning will hold off printing any new copies during this process, though any copies stocked at wholesalers or retailers will keep being sold.

For the revision, you might be tempted to skip getting a proof because you figure you don't need it—but if you're a beginner, or if the changes are major, I don't recommend this. You might also be tempted to skip it just to get your book back into distribution as soon as possible—but since proofs are delivered overnight, this saves only a day or two, so it makes little sense.

Now, you notice that when I talked about time required, I said "normally." There's one instance in which you can run into significant or even indefinite delay. Ironically, it's when your book is selling very well.

The problem arises because of Lightning's protocol for handling revisions. When you submit your files, your rep has to pull your book out of distribution and keep it that way while the files are processed and the proof is out for approval. But when she goes to do that, if she sees that the book has orders waiting, she can't pull the book till they've been filled.

So, your rep waits till the next day and tries again. The orders she saw the day before have now been filled, but . . . there are new orders that have arrived in the meantime. So, again, she's unable to pull the book.

The next day . . . . Well, for *most* books there will eventually be a break in the orders. But for the most popular, this cycle can just go on and on. Each day, there will be new orders waiting to be filled that prevent your rep from halting distribution and sending your files on for processing.

Meanwhile, Amazon gets a "Revision Submitted" message from the Lightning feed. Even though the book can still be ordered—and even though Amazon itself may still be successfully ordering it—Amazon takes this as a sign of impeded availability.

As long as Amazon has stock of the book or sees actual (not virtual) stock at Ingram, that's not a problem. But as soon as that stock is gone, Amazon changes the book's availability from "in stock" to something like 1–3 weeks. In another few days, it may say 2–5 weeks. And finally, "temporarily unavailable." At that point, of course, customers are being strongly discouraged, and the book is losing many sales—but not necessarily enough to let your rep get it into revision.

The upshot is, while you're waiting for a revision that may never go through, you might be losing hundreds or even thousands of dollars. This standoff may continue till you decide you simply can't afford to make the change you planned and tell your rep to cancel the revision. (This is not just theoretical. I have twice tried and failed to replace my old, poorly-executed cover for *The Business of Writing for Children*.)

I wish I could pull a simple solution out of my hat for you, but I can't. For instance, you can't just withdraw a book from distribution *before* submitting a revision, because this generates the very same problems. But if you get really desperate, here are some not-very-satisfactory ways to try to break the cycle.

• Cancel the revision and wait for a slower sales period before trying again.

• Cancel the revision, make the book returnable, and hope that induces Ingram to actually stock your book instead of ordering copies only as needed.

• Supply the book to Amazon through Amazon Advantage, then suspend the title in that program when the revision is complete at Lightning.

• Supply the book to Amazon through CreateSpace, then when ready, use the book's settings to turn off selling to Amazon. (Meanwhile, CreateSpace will have replaced your cover image on Amazon and submitted your book to Search Inside—but if that's not what you want, you can probably fix either of those later.)

Note: Setting up the book at either Advantage or Create-Space, even for temporary sales, really is a last resort. It will likely cause "vendor of record" problems, where Amazon will no longer recognize Lightning as the primary supplier of your book. While this won't stop Amazon from buying your book from Ingram, Amazon may no longer realize it can also order from Lightning, and it may ignore data changes of yours sent to it by either Lightning or Ingram. If you need to correct this, you *might* be able to do it by asking Amazon to note Lightning Source as your book's vendor of record.

Of course, if you get even close to the point of considering any of these measures, you should also be complaining to Lightning. Someday, they really will have to fix this! And really, all it would take is delinking order acceptance and fulfillment. In other words, it should be possible to fill outstanding orders while refusing new ones.

By the way, another solution is sometimes suggested but would *not* work: continuing to print and ship the current version of a book while a revision is in process. Understandably, Lightning's agreements with Amazon and other booksellers prohibit it from doing that. No one wants a book on the verge of being outdated!

Again, *most* books will eventually be pulled from distribution without any special effort on your part, even if it's not as soon as you'd like. So, don't let the potential risk keep you from trying to revise your book.

Be aware, though, that it's not just new book files that can trigger the cycle. Distribution must be halted to make any change in basic book data as well. Your book can get caught in revision hell for nothing more than the attempted correction of a typo in Lightning's listing.

So, if you do have any such change to make, do it as early as possible in the book's life cycle. Once a book gets popular, the tiniest fix can become very, very expensive. At that point, you may be better off leaving it as is at Lightning and instead fixing it at Ingram or just at individual retailers.

Consider Price Changes

At times, you may need to tinker with your book's price, discount, returnability, and/or distribution. On Lightning's Title Information page for your book, click on "Request Price Change." This will display a form with a list of every country where you've agreed that Lightning can distribute your books, whether or not you're currently allowing that *particular* book to be sold there.

If you *are* allowing it to be sold in a country, the checkbox next to the country name will be checked, and you'll see the current price and terms—and you can then go ahead and edit them. If you *don't* see all that but *do* want to allow sales in that country, just check the box and fill in the rest. (To *cancel* the book's distribution in a country, though, you'll have to contact your Client Services Rep.)

If you change any price on the form by over 30%, the form warns you and demands an explanation, with a threat of being turned down if Lightning isn't satisfied. Seriously! The explanations you can choose are "Negative publisher compensation" (meaning you're losing money), "Not generating enough revenue for the book," and "Not generating enough sales for the book." Oddly, there's no choice for "I goofed," which is the real reason I needed the change that generated this warning.

The form will show you the exact date your changes should go into effect. This will be set for the end of the current statement month, to simplify bookkeeping. As an option, you can choose a later month's end. Note that you *must* select a later date if you're already within five days of the current month's end.

When you're finished, click on "Submit." If you change your mind later but still more than five days before the effective date, you can return to the form. Edit further or click "Cancel" beside a country's row, then submit again. Just to make sure that's clear: After canceling a change, you must submit the entire form again for it to go through!

Unlike other metadata changes at Lightning, changes through this form do *not* require a halt in distribution, so you don't have to worry about postponement or complication. For that reason, using this form is the *only* safe way to add market info. You don't ever want it to be added manually by a rep or anyone else at Lightning.

Changes made through the form are nowadays mostly automated, so they go through pretty reliably—though you should still go back after the effective date to check on them. Ingram, on the other hand, is not quite as dependable. After a change goes into effect at Lightning, it may take anywhere from another day to another week to show up at Ingram, and it may even get lost entirely—especially if the price is being lowered. If that happens, complain to both Lightning and Ingram.

While Ingram might be slow or erratic at picking up price changes at Lightning, Baker & Taylor seems to ignore them completely. To make the same changes at B&T, send notice to

PC@btol.com

You might give the change to Bowker and Nielsen as well, though prices they show are non-binding, since they're not used directly for buying. Any such informational listings can be handled either before or after the official date of change.

At this writing, a change in list price at Lightning shows up in the book's listing on Amazon within a few days. The matching change in Amazon's price, though, can take up to two weeks to appear. During this lag time, Amazon will sell the book either at the same price as before or at the new list price, whichever is lower. (Amazon no longer adds a temporary "sourcing fee" when the new list price goes below the old selling price.)

Note that Amazon applies the new price not only to book copies it has yet to buy but also to copies it has in stock—even if it loses money on them. Probably this balances out, with Amazon gaining about as much money on some price changes as it loses on others. In any case, this practice alone shows clearly that Amazon cares more about profit overall than from individual book copies or even titles.

Adding Distribution Options

From time to time, Lightning adds distribution options for new countries. For you to take advantage of one, you'll have to sign a new agreement or amendment. (If it isn't sent to you automatically, you can request it from one of your reps.)

At that time, you may be asked to supply the prices and terms for your books in the new market. Don't do this! It will become a metadata change that requires temporarily removing each book from distribution. And with Lightning's current issues regarding that (as discussed in the section on price changes), the time of unavailability could last indefinitely.

Instead, just say you'll add the data later through the Web site. Then do that by going to Lightning's Title Information page for each book, clicking on "Request Price Change," and filling in the new slots that will appear for that option. Your book will be made available in the new country at the end of the month with no interruption in availability elsewhere.

And if you're already stuck in a cycle of unavailability from an addition initiated by your rep? Just cancel it, then add the data online.

Consider Double Sourcing

Lightning Source may be the only POD provider you ever need. If you're lucky, it *will* be.

On the other hand, you may find that a particular book will benefit from the offerings of another company as well. In that case, you might wish to *double source*—make it available from both Lightning and the other provider, in the same edition and with the same ISBN.

For instance, at this writing, I have two novels and one illustrated children's book that are double sourced at Amazon's CreateSpace. I prefer CreateSpace's non-glossy type for the novels, and it has a better trim size and more suitable production requirements for the children's book. So, my motives here are more aesthetic than economic—though at higher page counts, CreateSpace's lower color print charges may yield slightly more profit than the greater discounts allowed by Lightning.

Another reason you might want to double source is to expand distribution. Lightning's is the widest you'll find, but that doesn't mean it covers all bases. For example, TextStream, Baker & Taylor's response to Lightning, may soon offer better access to Borders and Borders.com. (For more on this provider, see "Learning About TextStream" in the appendix.)

Double sourcing, though, comes with its own costs in complication. For one thing, you can't be sure where Amazon will order your book. This is true even when double sourcing with CreateSpace. Though you'd think Amazon would always order from its own company, CreateSpace is still young and has grabbed a lot more business than it can handle. So, if it falls behind, it looks for a quick way to supply your book—and for any book also with Lightning, that means drop shipping by Ingram.

When you double source, book revisions and price changes must be carefully coordinated between sources. Otherwise, you could wind up selling two different versions at the same time, or have your book sold at two different prices. As you can imagine, this coordination can be quite tricky, due to varying lead times, stocking, and the general cussedness of bulky systems. Books likely to undergo changes, then, are not good candidates for double sourcing.

And Heaven help you if you want to double source *and* accept returns! Be prepared for books to be returned to a different source than the one that printed them—especially if you shut off returns at just one source.

Double sourcing can certainly be a help in some cases, but do it only with good reason and with awareness of problems it might create. Otherwise, you set yourself up for needless trouble, and possibly for loss of profit as well.*

And please don't think of avoiding such problems by having two separate editions of your book, each with its own ISBN, with one edition at each source. Both will wind up on Amazon, where sales rank will be split between them, hurting both.

By the way, did I mention triple sourcing? . . .

---

* One reason to double source that is *not* good is the fear that Amazon will stop ordering all Lightning books. This fear has caused a number of Lightning self publishers to double source with CreateSpace at much worse terms, and in that way lose substantial amounts of money. Though Amazon did at one point make this threat, it has since backed off from its position and in any case does not seem to have ever meant to apply it to independent self publishers. Besides, if Amazon ever did stop, you could give your books to CreateSpace at that time.

Turn Down Buyouts

If your book is successful on Amazon, you may one day get an email asking if you'd be interested in selling the publishing rights to a traditional publisher. This kind of offer is certainly flattering, and many self publishers would jump at it. But a little reflection might lead to a different decision.

Whether you should accept really boils down to what your goals are. Do you want to get your book in front of as many readers as possible? Do you crave the prestige and affirmation of being published by someone else? Is your book merely a platform from which to attract more lucrative business?

If any of these are true, then selling the rights to your book may well be the best choice. But it probably *won't* be best if you want to make the most possible money *from your book.*

The truth is, *if your book is already successful,* you can probably do better with it on your own. That's because, even if the other publisher can sell more copies, it probably can't sell enough to make up for your decreased percentage of profit. In ballpark figures, it would have to sell *five to ten times more—* and that's simply not likely.

You've done the hard work. Don't be so quick to give away the profit.

If you decline, the publisher may try to be "reasonable" about it. What if you kept your edition and let them put out their own, aimed at bookstores? Don't fall for this. Any other edition of your book will wind up on Amazon, competing with yours and decreasing your sales. A hardcover edition might not be so bad, but the publisher will not likely accept being limited to that.

If you do decide to sell the rights to your book, for whatever reason, at least make sure there's a clear and plausible way for you to get them back. It's not enough for your contract to say you can reclaim the rights if the book goes "out of print." Today, with print on demand, a book *never* has to go out of print.

Instead, make sure the contract defines "out of print" as sales under a specific number of copies per year. Also make sure that figure is large enough for your comfort. And try to make sure the return of rights to you is *automatic*. You don't want to be required to go through a lengthy, frustrating process of requesting the reversion and then waiting for the publisher to get around to granting it—if it ever does.

Publish More Books

If you're reading this book, it's likely you've already caught the publishing bug. For those of us afflicted, publishing one book is simply not enough. Nor is two. Once we experience the thrill of bringing books into the world, we just can't stop publishing.

But the question always is, what should the next book be? And the one after that?

You have two basic choices. One is to publish books that *complement* the ones before. Publishing a number of books on related topics or in the same genre can greatly boost the sales of each. For instance, my first book on reader's theater sold much better once I had two more in place.

The other choice is to *diversify*. Subject fields and genres grow more or less popular, and publishing in more than one can provide a financial buffer. At this point, I publish books in the fields of writing and publishing, reader's theater, music, crafts, and children's books, among others. Even week to week, I'll sometimes see interest in one subject rise and in another one fall. As I've said before, you can accommodate divergent books by creating new *imprints* as divisions of your company, though you'll keep things much simpler by sticking to one publishing name.

So far, I've been talking as if your additional published books had to be written by you (or maybe your spouse). But of course, that's not the case. Some self publishers enjoy the process so much, they wind up reaching out to publish books by others as well. This can certainly be a rewarding way to go, but I suggest you think three times before rushing in.

Remember, when you publish someone else, you will be bound to that author for the life of your agreement. You'll have to deal with that author's perhaps wild expectations and misunderstandings of the publishing process. You'll have to deliver the book in a timely fashion. And then you'll have to know exactly how many copies of the book you've sold, and pay promptly on that basis—perhaps for the rest of your life, or even longer.

If you do decide to publish someone else, it can be a challenge to figure out fair terms. For instance, traditional royalties from major publishers range between about 5% and 10% of the list price, while the traditional profit margin that those publishers aim for is around 10% of list. But how do you figure it with a Lightning book, where easily half the list price can be available to split between publisher profit and author earnings? And then how do you deal with it if some copies are sold through more traditional channels, in which the profit margin is so small?

Here are tentative terms I've worked out for publishing a friend of my own, adapting them from earlier agreements of mine with illustrators. (An illustrator who has equal billing with the author—as on a children's picture book—would get half the amounts and percentages shown below.) You're welcome to use them as a starting point in constructing your own author contract.

Rights granted: All publication rights, worldwide, in any language, in any medium. (These would be the rights granted to me by the author. But the author would remain the primary rights holder, and the copyright would be in her name.)

Rights return: On request, after 10 years from publication date.

Advance: None. (Or you could pay a nominal sum to show good faith.)

Royalty: 50% of net receipts for publisher's licensed sales; 10% of list price for publisher's direct sales. (*Licensed sales* includes any sales through Lightning or any other POD printer/distributor. *Net receipts* would be the amount I actually receive—for instance, Lightning's publisher compensation payments. *Publisher's direct sales* means any sales directly to booksellers or readers.)

Rights split: 50% of net receipts. (This would apply when I sell "subsidiary" rights to other publishers to reprint, translate, adapt, and so on.)

Payment schedule: Payment for sales from January 1 to December 31 will be sent by April 1. (I actually like to make this kind of payment in January, but the April 1 date would give me some leeway in case I need to wait for sales data or for payment due to me.)

Author copies: 10 copies of publisher's print edition in each binding. Author can buy additional copies at publisher's cost, including shipping, with prepayment.

As you may know, author contracts can get quite long and complex. I prefer to keep agreements to a single page, leaving the rest to mutual trust, respect, and negotiation. Where that doesn't seem feasible, I'd frankly rather not get involved. Of course, that approach may not work if you search for publishable books outside your circle of friends.

Another source of material that attracts small publishers is public domain books—in other words, books old enough to have passed out of copyright. The attraction is that you don't have to pay royalties or deal with an author in any way.

In former days, this niche was overwhelmingly dominated by Dover Publications—but now, with print on demand, an army of other publishers has jumped into the fray. In general, their strategy is to publish as many books as possible, as cheaply as possible, and make a little money from each. Book interiors may be assembled from scanned pages or from electronic texts prepared with OCR (optical character recognition). Covers may be nicely designed or generic.

My advice is to not try to compete in this field, for one simple reason: Too many publishers have already piled onto this bandwagon. It has gotten to the point that Amazon has started purposely ignoring many duplicate editions in search results.

Still, you may have one or two favorite books that are out of print and have been overlooked by the publishing hordes and that you'd dearly love to make available again. If you do, check carefully to make sure they are out of copyright. Neither Lightning nor any bookseller will check this for you, and you could be liable for legal action if you're wrong.

In the U.S., changes in copyright law have made the copyright situation more and more complex, as well as more and more unfavorable to reprinters. But here are the basics for works originally published in the U.S., good for anytime up through the year 2018.

• 1964 or after—Anything with a copyright date in this period is still protected.

• 1923 to 1963—Anything copyrighted in this period *may* still be protected, depending on whether the copyright was ever renewed. The only way to find out is to conduct a copyright search.

• 1922 or before—Anything published in this period is definitely out of copyright. Fair game. Free and clear.

To verify this, find details, or get updates, visit the U.S. Copyright Office at

www.copyright.gov

For the ambiguous period of 1923 to 1963, you can pay the Copyright Office to conduct a search for a renewal, or you can do it yourself online. Stanford University maintains a database of renewals at

collections.stanford.edu/copyrightrenewals

For general help and more links, see "Information About the Catalog of Copyright Entries," an article on The Online Books Page from the University of Pennsylvania, at

onlinebooks.library.upenn.edu/cce

Texts of a huge number of public domain books can now be found free on the Web. But if you consider using any, note that the transcription may be in copyright even when the original work is not. Be careful to check any terms of use associated with the text.

What if the work was originally published outside the U.S.? If you're publishing in the U.S. yourself, then U.S. law applies to all works you might wish to use—but the protection given by that law may still differ. Works from some countries are not legally protected at all! For most countries, though, figure that anything published in 1923 or after is protected, while anything published earlier is not.

Copyright protection in the rest of the world can be both simpler and more problematic. The most common arrangement is automatic protection of the work—published or unpublished—for the life of the author plus 75 years. This means you don't have to hunt for copyright registration or even a work's initial publication date, but you do have to know that the author died more than 75 years ago.

Unfortunately, in the case of an obscure author, tracking down a death date may be next to impossible. You may have to make a judgment call or simply forget the book. (Personally, I'd rather have some future publisher resurrect my work than leave it in obscurity for fear of accidentally infringing the rights of my heirs.)

A U.S. publisher can easily run into a situation in which a work is protected overseas but not in the U.S. You can still publish it, but you must instruct Lightning to distribute it *in the U.S. only*. Your U.S. book might still wind up sold overseas—for instance, by Amazon Marketplace sellers—but as long as you're not selling there yourself, you're not violating any rights.

If you're determined to reprint a less obscure work, see my suggestions for this in *Aiming at Amazon*. But also make sure you check the current situation on Amazon, which is becoming less and less friendly to such publishing.

Yet another tempting opportunity for small publishers is anthologies—collections of works by a variety of authors. Depending on how you handle this, it can be a rewarding experience or a nightmare. Specifically, if you approach large publishers for permissions, you are likely to face exorbitant fees and also time limits on usage—limits developed with traditional publishing in mind rather than print on demand.

The last thing you want is to have to renegotiate and re-purchase all your permissions at outrageous prices every few years, and at intervals that vary for different pieces! Instead, aim to deal directly with authors who own their rights. Authors are almost always more reasonable than publishers, usually accepting a fair and affordable one-time fee.

If you do decide to seek permissions from large publishers, make sure you state the exact rights you need and include details on your book and your marketing projections—enough so the publisher can judge what your book might earn and how much of its content will be made up of the requested piece. Also include a copy of the text you're asking to print.

Keep in mind that most fees and terms you're quoted are negotiable. But even after being lowered, some fees may not be affordable, and sometimes you'll run into a simple no. Prepare for that by having on hand more material than you need.

For further advice on permissions for anthologies, see my article "The Perils of Permissions" in the section "The Inside Story" on my Kidwriting Page.

www.aaronshep.com/kidwriter

Aging on Amazon

Books, like people, have lives. They grow, mature, decline, sometimes rally, and eventually die. Their lives may be short or long, but you can't count on any book to last forever. On the other hand, Amazon and POD have greatly increased a book's life expectancy and have induced many a resurrection.

Let's take a look at some of the factors in the long-term prospects of a POD book on Amazon. We'll start with factors adding to growth.

• Amazon keeps growing in the number of book-buying customers—even if not as rapidly as before.

• Your book on Amazon develops relationships over time. As I've said, it takes about a full year for a book to reach its full potential, as it builds a position within Amazon's systems of referral and recommendation.

• Amazon gets smarter and smarter about selling books. Through its ever-developing systems, it keeps getting better at connecting readers with the books they'll want to buy.

• Amazon invents new ways for authors and publishers to help sell their books. And some are even effective!

• *You* keep getting smarter. As you learn more and gain experience, you get better at marketing your book, both on Amazon and off. (Or let's hope so.)

And now, factors contributing to decline:

• Amazon keeps growing in the number of books it carries—due to their increased life expectancy, plus the explosion in small-scale publishing, including self publishing. So, the sales pie, though getting larger, gets cut into slices that are relatively smaller and smaller.

• Your competitors' books too are developing relationships. The same systems that help sell your book are helping sell theirs. A relationship with your book may draw away buyers.

• Amazon gets smarter and smarter about selling *other* people's books too. And as it becomes more effective in marketing *all* books, any lead you've developed through your own smart marketing becomes narrower.

• Amazon removes old ways for authors and publishers to help sell their books, or allows them to fall into disrepair. And some were even effective!

• You have other things to do. You can't keep focused on one book forever. So, you may miss new marketing opportunities or simply not have time to pursue them.

And finally, factors that could affect a book either way:

• Your book's content is more or less timely—ranging from quickly becoming obsolete to remaining relevant for generations.

• Topics, slants, genres, and so on become more or less popular. Some reader interests can be measured in days. Others, in decades. And once they're gone, they can always revive.

• A string of good or bad Customer Reviews, deserved or not, may permanently change your book's prospects.

• The economy might go boom or bust, inciting more or less book buying.

The upshot is that even a successful book may sink well before you'd expect or may sell well for the rest of your life. You can't be sure exactly where on the spectrum it will fall. The outcome, though, will at least be influenced by your choice of content, the quality of your book, and the effectiveness of your marketing.

Good luck to you!

Appendix

Where to Get Help

I'm always glad to receive feedback on my books, but I'm afraid I can't offer consulting, mentoring, or other private guidance, paid or unpaid. (Strangely enough, I actually make my living from publishing, not from talking about it!)

For personal help and to keep up to date, please join the Yahoo group pod_publishers. That's where I hang out, myself, so you might find me answering your questions anyway.

groups.yahoo.com/group/pod_publishers

My Publishing Page has a number of resources for self publishers, including my Publishing Blog, with which I try to keep my readers up to date. To find consultants who can help you work with Lightning Source, see "Other Publishing Resources."

www. newselfpublishing.com

Though *Aiming at Amazon* was among the first books to describe a publishing plan based on Lightning Source, it was actually the second. First out of the gate was *Print-on-Demand Book Publishing,* by my friend Morris Rosenthal. Morris continues to offer his always-interesting insights on publishing old and new on his Web site and especially on his Self Publishing 2.0 blog.

www.fonerbooks.com/cornered.htm

While I hope *POD for Profit* tells you most of what you need to know about Lightning Source and print on demand from the perspective of a self publisher, you might also be interested to know about it from the viewpoint of traditional publishing. For that, the Book Industry Study Group offers the booklet *Digital Book Printing for Dummies*. Though published through Wiley in the style of its popular For Dummies line, it's actually an industry resource with numerous industry contributors and sponsors—including Lightning Source—and available only through the Web sites of the BISG and the Independent Book Publishers Association. (The latter offers free shipping.)

www.bisg.org
www.ibpa-online.org

For ongoing coverage of Lightning Source and the publishing world in general, I recommend reading *Publishers Weekly* and/or its daily email bulletin, *PW Daily*. It will alert you to trends that may be helpful for long-term strategy and will help ward off misconceptions such as often circulate among self publishers.

www.publishersweekly.com

Lightning itself offers a bewildering array of helpful documents and resources, viewable online and off, some more current than others, scattered around the site. Many are accessible only *before* you log in, from the File Creation and Tutorials menus on the home page. The most important document here is the "File Creation Guide." It's the most comprehensive technical guide that Lightning offers on file preparation.

Other resources are accessed from the page that appears after login, called "My Lightning Account at a Glance." Click on "FAQs" for answers to common questions. Click the links under "How Tos" to view or download several PDF documents.

Finally, go to the My Account menu on that page and click on "Operating Manuals & Contract Documents." This brings you to the page with the most essential and authoritative of Lightning's documents. Most important, be sure to download and *study* the POD operating manual for your country. This describes in detail your business relationship with Lightning, including pricing, and provides much technical guidance as well.

The *Lightning Source Global Newsletter,* a not-really-biannual newsletter on global development, is posted by Lightning UK at

www.lsi-news.com

iPage Publisher Accounts

On request from any of its publishers, Lightning Source will arrange an account on ipage, Ingram's Web portal. The kind of account offered, though, is a modified *bookseller* or *retailer* account.

In the old days, before that was available, Lightning publishers could instead apply to ipage directly and receive a more powerful *publisher* or *supplier* account. For the sake of those old-timers lucky enough to have one, here's a discussion of the extra things you can see and do with it.

When searching, you can switch the search database from "Ingram Active" to "Ingram Extended." This will let you perform any kind of search among *all* books listed, even those not currently available for ordering. (You can set this and other search preferences in your User Settings.)

On your book's product detail page, a publisher account will let you see figures on sales and "demand"—the number of times a book's details have been accessed either on ipage or by other means. At least, that's what the demand figures are *supposed* to show. According to my relentless analyst friend Morris Rosenthal, Ingram's demand figures haven't made sense by that definition since 2002. So, exactly what they now mean or are good for is anyone's guess.

You'll see that ipage gives sales and demand figures for the current month broken down by distribution center, plus overall monthly and yearly figures for up to the last five years. Like the stocking quantities elsewhere on this page, these figures are updated nightly (except Friday's sales don't show up till Monday).

Keep in mind that ipage sales figures are only for copies sold *through Ingram*. Amazon and BN.com do order through

Ingram, but they also order directly from Lightning, and so does Baker & Taylor. None of those direct Lightning orders are included in ipage figures. The most you can tell from ipage is roughly how many copies of your book are sold through special orders. Subtract that from your Lightning figures, and you'll also see roughly how many are being ordered for stock.

At the level of account given to Lightning publishers, you can see these sales and demand figures for your books, and for your books only. If you *don't* see the figures for one of your books, it generally means the book has not been properly associated with that account and you need to get that fixed. But note that, if you have multiple imprints, you would need a separate account to see the figures for each—and if you don't have that set up already, it's probably too late.

Another major benefit of a publisher account is access to SUPPLiWAY, Ingram's online system for managing book info. This can sometimes be used to add info that ipage and Amazon will display but that Lightning does not collect from you. You can also try correcting basic listing errors from here. That isn't supposed to work for Lightning publishers, but at least some-times, it does.

With SUPPLiWAY, you can also replace the displayed cover image supplied by Lightning. Your new image should show up on ipage within a few days. In the past, I've also used this as a simple way to replace images at Amazon—but in a later test, this didn't work. Be aware, too, that any new cover image generated by Lightning will replace yours on ipage, so you may have to submit again.

To reach SUPPLiWAY, click on the "Information Mgmt." tab and then the "SUPPLiWAY Product Management" link. Run a search for your title or titles. You can search on your publisher prefix here as a "Product Code." If you have separate accounts for different imprints, make sure you're in the right account.

From the list of results, click on a book's Edit button—*not* its title—to bring up a one-page form. As usual, most fields are optional—but note that some data is mandatory here that Lightning didn't ask for, and your submission won't be accepted without it. Also, the form doesn't show all data already submitted—for instance, your book description won't be visible. Remember too that Ingram can't handle a long subtitle, so don't try to enter one on this form.

The "Add" buttons on this form act differently from the ones you may have used in your Bowker My Identifiers account and elsewhere. In My Identifiers, the buttons added more fields for you to fill in. In SUPPLiWAY, they take the data you've entered, add it to the database, and empty the fields again for additional entries. For instance, current authors/contributors are listed on the SUPPLiWAY form *below* both the "Add" button and the fields used for entering data on new ones.

The form also lets you upload your book cover image. You specify a file on your computer that will then be uploaded *only* when you submit the entire form. Note that the upload will increase the time it takes for SUPPLiWAY to return an acknowledgment page.

The form is submitted when you hit the "Update Information" button at the bottom. This sends it for manual processing, which might take as long as a week. During that time, you will *not* be able to edit what you sent. If you return to the form before processing is complete, you'll see only what was there before your changes.

Some Lightning publishers have used SUPPLiWAY to list books on ipage and Amazon before submitting the books to Lightning. But I don't recommend this, because Ingram can become confused as to where to get the book. Until you get this cleared up, your book will have poor availability on Amazon and won't be available to most booksellers at all.

Though ipage's publisher account is the more powerful, a bookseller account has its own advantages. For example, only a bookseller account shows the discounts Ingram is offering to retailers. So, even if you have a publisher account, you might ask Lightning for a bookseller account as well, allowing you to use each at different times.

Working with BowkerLink

The word from Bowker is that all online submissions of info for Books in Print will eventually go through My Identifiers accounts at Bowker's new Identifier Services. But for now, if that's not where you obtained your ISBNs, the old BowkerLink site is probably still the portal for you. That's at

www.bowkerlink.com

If you don't already have an account there, I suggest you set one up at least one month before you plan to launch your book. To do that, click on the site's registration link for new users. You'll select your publishing name from a database and then be given a simple form to fill out online. If the site can't find your publishing name—as it might not, for example, if your ISBNs are from outside the U.S.—or if you have any other trouble, write to one of these addresses.

BIP.BowkerLink@bowker.com
DataAcquisition@bowker.com

And if the problem is a missing name, be sure your message includes that name *and* your ISBN prefix.

Once you get confirmation of your account, you can customize it and manage your publisher listing. Click on "My Account," then "Detailed Account Information," and you should find a "Time Out" preference. Select the longest time available, so the system won't bump you while you're struggling with the site's forms.

Next, go to the section for publisher info. As your distributors, list "Lightning Source, Incorporated" and "Lightning

Source UK Limited." *Do not try to add Ingram.* That's a wholesaler, not a distributor, and will not be accepted.

Some self publishers might be tempted not to offer the distributor info, in an attempt to escape a supposed stigma of print on demand. But this is not the place to do that. Books in Print is used largely to locate books for special orders for bookstores, schools, and libraries, and listing Lightning Source will tell most Bowker users that your books can be obtained from major wholesalers. If you leave that out, the person ordering may try to order from you direct—and probably one of the last things you want is to fill orders for one or two copies.

Another means to avoid direct orders is to minimize the contact info Bowker displays for you. Remove or hide any telephone number or email address. If you must include a street address, mask it as being for "editorial mailing" or such. Giving a Web site address is fine, because you can make your site tell booksellers they can't order direct!

If you see a field that's marked as required but is empty, do *not* assume you need to fill it in. Sometimes a field is required only in the context of that section of the form. If Bowker really needs it, you'll get an error message when you submit, along with the chance to fix it.

If you're publishing under an imprint name besides your main publishing name, you'll have to email a request for the additional name to be set up. Send your request, along with your ISBN prefix, to Bowker's Publishers Authority Database department, at

PAD@bowker.com

You'll then be able to select the name when submitting book info.

Note that a BowkerLink account does *not* let you look up anyone's books but your own. Sorry!

As soon as your files are uploaded at Lightning, it's time to submit your title to BowkerLink, if you haven't already. To reach the Title Information form, log onto the site and click on "Add Title." Here are things to remember to make the form as painless as possible.

- Only some fields are required, as marked.
- Start from the top of each page and work down. Skipping around may confuse the interactive form.
- Click on "Additional Title Information" at the bottom of the first page to reach the second.
- Complete both pages, then click "Finish and Save!" Until then, you can use the page-bottom links to move safely back and forth between pages—but do *not* try to upload a cover image before saving, or you'll lose everything you've entered!
- Saving the form will close it, but you can retrieve it for editing or for cover image upload by clicking on "View Pending Transactions."
- If you've given your book both long and short subtitles, use the long one here. Bowker will accept a subtitle that's just as long as the one you give Amazon. (Longer, in fact.)
- For a paperback, "Binding" would be "Trade Paper."
- Don't list contributors who are not shown on the title page of your book. For instance, if you hired a freelance editor, do *not* list him or her as "Editor" on the form.
- For "Title Status," say "Active Record."
- For "Publication Date," provide the same date you gave Lightning—not the date you're giving to reviewers, if that differs. (You can switch it later, if you like, once both dates have passed.)
- For "Price Type," say "Retail Price."
- The U.S. distributor would be Lightning Source. (It should appear here as an option if you previously entered it in your publisher info, as I advised before—but it may take some

time after that to show up, because the info must be processed manually.)

• In most cases, the "target market" would be "Trade."

• Typically, a Lightning book should be listed at Bowker with U.K. info too—so click on "Add Additional Geographic Markets," select "United Kingdom," and enter price info in British pounds, with Lightning UK as the distributor.

• At this writing, Lightning is based in the U.S. and the U.K. only—so don't add other markets unless you live and sell there yourself.

• For copyright year, enter the year printed in the book, whether or not it matches the publication date you gave.

Your Title Information submission is normally processed by the next business day, so you can return then to check it, and if needed, to revise it. You don't have to enter anything in the title search form—just click the "Search" button, and Bowker will list any books it has for you, letting you select one.

For cover image upload, you'll see a link in search results and another on the book's Title Information form. (Remember to "Finish and Save!" before leaving a Title Information form you're working on.) If you have trouble submitting your image online, wait a day or two after entering your book info, then email the image to

BowkerLink.Covers@bowker.com

Or for 10 or more, send them on disc to

R. R. Bowker
Attn: Data Services—Images
630 Central Avenue
New Providence, NJ 07974

Images are processed once a week. New images will appear online right after that, while replacements can take a couple more days.

As I said before, Amazon in its early days drew book data automatically from Bowker for its listings, and later it used Bowker as needed to manually verify book data—but neither is true any longer. Nothing you submit to Bowker will automatically show up on Amazon or even be visible to it. More specifically, you *cannot* use an early entry at BowkerLink to make Amazon prelist your book.

BN.com, on the other hand, does draw from Bowker. A book you list there should appear on BN.com within a couple of days.

By the way, whether you get your account from Bowker-Link or Identifier Services, the same username and password will work on both sites. So, feel free to poke around your My Identifiers account to see how the new site is coming along and whether it offers any advantages to you.

Learning About TextStream

Lightning Source will remain the dominant player in the POD industry for the foreseeable future, but one other provider is trying to imitate its success. Just as Lightning is connected to Ingram, the largest U.S. wholesaler, TextStream is a division of the second largest, Baker & Taylor. It's a reboot of Replica Books, which was almost as old as Lightning but dwindled through neglect. Now, as TextStream, it's coming back with a vengeance—or at least trying to.

A new POD center opened at a Baker & Taylor distribution facility in September 2009, operated for the wholesaler by the international printing company R. R. Donnelly. Plans are to show all books as always in stock in the B&T catalog, in a system similar to Ingram's virtual stocking.

TextStream publishers are allowed to set their own prices, discounts, and returns policies, just as at Lightning. Most printing prices too are comparable to Lightning's. But Text-Stream has some capabilities that Lightning does not. For instance, page counts in black-and-white paperbacks can go as low as 24 pages, and binding options include spiral. More importantly, TextStream's color offerings seem to raise the bar significantly from Lightning's, with more trim sizes, more binding options, better paper grades, and lower prices.

What's more, TextStream can be somewhat more lenient with its production requirements than Lightning is—and for now at least, self publishers seem more warmly welcomed.

Though TextStream's distribution won't be as wide as Lightning's anytime soon, it may offer one nice advantage: better access to both Borders and Borders.com. For wholesale book supply, Borders—the bricks-and-mortar part—relies mainly on Baker & Taylor, which has spotty listing and no stocking of Lightning books. So, Borders clerks routinely tell customers that Lightning books are "unavailable" or "out of print." Books from TextStream, on the other hand, will hopefully all be seen listed at B&T as available.

Borders.com—the online part—knows about *some* Lightning books, but only ones that have made it to B&T's database—and it refuses to sell any that are on short discount. But with TextStream, *all* books should sell on Borders.com, even if on short discount—at least to begin with. Meanwhile, B&T's listings should also get TextStream books onto both Amazon.com and BN.com.

But you may notice I'm qualifying a lot of these statements. At this writing, TextStream looks promising, but it's really just starting up. Like Replica before it, it's still understaffed and under-automated. Its documentation is a mess—a contradictory jumble of new instructions and old ones inherited from Replica days. It has no Web site yet for clients.

Most important, though, Baker & Taylor's virtual stocking is not yet accepted by Amazon, Borders, or other retailers. That's most likely because TextStream's delivery times to B&T are still several days, compared to Lightning's overnight to Ingram. The upshot is that Borders.com currently lists these books with availability times stretching into weeks, while Amazon and BN.com, if they list the books at all, show them as out of stock. TextStream has promised to address this early in 2010, but its record to date gives no assurance of success.*

Still, TextStream bears close watching, especially as a potential complement to Lightning in your publishing plans. Until TextStream puts up its own Web site, find basic info at

www.btol.com/supplier_textstream.cfm

---

* To test current availability yourself, you can check this ISBN, which is for a book only at TextStream: 9780938497295.

The Stigma of POD*

Nowadays, there's an odd belief circulating that self pub-lishing a book as print on demand will keep it out of book-stores. Actually, the opposite is true.

Let's follow Susan Self-Publisher as she visits her local Barnes & Noble, book held proudly in hand. Her mission is to convince Michael Manager to schedule a book signing for her. She's pleased to find that Michael *is* interested, and she waits happily as he goes to check the store computer. But Michael returns to tell her apologetically he's not allowed to order POD books for special events. Susan goes home fuming over this discrimination and bewildered as to how Michael could know her book was POD. (These names have been changed to protect your innocence.)

But Susan is looking at this from the wrong angle. She doesn't understand she has run smack into a major advantage of POD, not a drawback. And Michael may not realize it either, or just not have time to explain.

You see, the actual B&N policy is that a store can't order a book for stocking or a special event unless the book has been reviewed and accepted by a nationwide B&N buyer. How does Michael know a book has been reviewed and accepted? The book is in the store computer. It doesn't get *into* the store computer unless it has been reviewed and accepted.

That is, unless the book is from Lightning Source, the kingpin of the POD industry. Lightning handles printing and distribution for thousands of independent self publishers and nearly every self publishing company in the U.S.—Lulu, AuthorHouse, iUniverse, Xlibris, you name it—including the

---

* This is an article from my Publishing Page, posted in January 2010.

one Susan signed with. And that's not to mention the traditional publishers that are increasingly coming to rely on it.

Barnes & Noble has a special arrangement with Lightning to list all its books in B&N's computers—meaning all the books handled by Lightning for the small and large publishers and self publishing companies it serves—and by far the greater number of those books have *not* been reviewed and accepted. All the ones *not* accepted are prominently labeled in the computer as Print on Demand. It's this label that tells Michael that Susan's book cannot be ordered for a special event.

But that's not why it's there. Susan's book is labeled Print on Demand so any clerk in any Barnes & Noble store will know *it can always be special ordered.*

In other words, the POD label is not the sign of discrimination Susan believes. On the contrary, it's what puts the book into the store computer in the first place and makes it available for special ordering throughout the chain! Without that, any customer asking for the book would be told it was unavailable, or just "out of print." Which is exactly what used to happen before B&N's computers started listing Lightning books.

Now, this is not to say Barnes and Noble likes POD. In general, it doesn't. That's because most POD books—including the ones from self publishing companies like Susan's—are sold to booksellers at reduced discounts and with returns disallowed. This means B&N generally can't make as much money on a POD book as on others. So, the policy that kept Michael from ordering Susan's book isn't discrimination, it's good business! (This is not to mention that many POD books are not up to professional standards, even with the additional paid services of a self publishing company.)

If Susan really wants an event at Michael's store, she can manage that without abandoning POD. She could leave her current self publishing company, find a new one that offers standard terms to booksellers, and put out a new edition. Or she could put it out while working directly with Lightning Source and set those terms herself.

In either case, she would then submit her book for review to B&N's Small Press Department. That department is quite happy to consider any POD book that is offered on standard terms and that can be ordered from a major wholesaler—which all Lightning books can, since they're listed by Lightning's sister company, Ingram, the largest book wholesaler in the U.S.

Of course, there's no guarantee the Small Press Department will accept Susan's book. And if it does, the terms that Susan has obligingly offered may lose her more than she gains. But all that's a different story.

OK, now let's follow Barbara Book-Lover into Borders, where she's going in search of Susan's book after reading about it online. Barbara doesn't find the book on the shelves, so she asks Clark Clerk, who looks it up in the store computer. (Oops! Forgot to change the names!)

Here in Borders, Clark doesn't see that the book is POD—in fact, he doesn't see the book at all. Borders has no direct relationship with Lightning, and the primary wholesaler it relies on is not Ingram but Baker & Taylor. As for B&T, it lists only *some* of Lightning's books and stocks almost none—and the data it sends to retailers includes only books in stock. So, Susan's book is not in the Borders store computer, and like B&N clerks in the past, Clark tells Barbara the book is out of print.

But unlike at B&N, Clark also tells Barbara she can have the store track down a used copy for her. Barbara decides to do this. Her request is then passed on to Clark Clerk, Sr., who handles special orders. (Good, I remembered to change that one.)

Unlike Clark Jr., Clark Sr. can check any number of sources, including Ingram. But like Michael over at B&N, he is under a constraint of his own—a strict Borders policy against backordering. In other words, if the book were listed at Ingram but shown as out of stock—even if clearly marked print on demand—Clark Sr. would have to ignore it.

But guess what? Susan's book—like *most* Lightning books—shows 100 copies in stock at Ingram. (All of them show *at least* 100.) Now, Clark Sr. has been around the bookstore a few times, and he knows well enough that those 100 copies are "virtual"—or in plain English, imaginary—and that they're a dead giveaway of POD. But that makes no difference to him. In fact, he's relieved to see that stock number, because *it allows him to order the book.* So, Susan makes the sale.

The hard truth is, self publishers have *always* had trouble getting books into bookstores, and especially into the chains. Far from keeping self publishers out, POD for the first time makes most self published books obtainable through almost every bookstore in the U.S.!

But all this skirts the most important point. The primary market for self publishers today is not bookstores at all. It's online booksellers, and particularly Amazon. And POD is by far the most efficient and profitable means to sell to that market.

So, look to where your sales *are,* not to where they are *not.* Truly, self publishers have never had it so good—and that's thanks to POD.

Author Online!

For updates and more resources,
visit Aaron Shepard's Publishing Page at

www. newselfpublishing.com

Index

About the Author

Aaron Shepard is a foremost proponent of the *new* business of profitable self publishing through print on demand, which he has practiced and helped develop since 1998. Unlike most authorities on self publishing, he makes the bulk of his living from his self-published books—not from consulting, speaking, freelance writing, or selling publishing services. In a parallel life, Aaron is an award-winning children's author with numerous picture books from publishers both large and small. He lives in Friday Harbor, Washington, in the San Juan Islands, with his wife and fellow author, Anne L. Watson.

How This Book Was Made

This book was made on a Mac. The pages were created in Microsoft Word, and the cover in Adobe InDesign. The author portrait was edited with Adobe Photoshop. PDF files were produced and processed with Adobe Acrobat Pro. The interior text font is 12-point Georgia with 15-point linespacing, and the cover typeface is Verdana.

Version History

1.0   March 2, 2010

Made in the USA
Lexington, KY
16 February 2012